S0-BFD-497

Building a Successful Business Plan:

Advice from the Experts

By the Editors of Socrates

SOCRATES
KNOW HOW TO DO MORE
AND SAVE

Socrates Media, LLC
227 West Monroe, Suite 500
Chicago, IL 60606
www.socrates.com

This publication is designed to provide accurate and authoritative information in regard to the subject matter covered. It is sold with the understanding that the publisher is not engaged in rendering legal, accounting or other professional service. If legal advice or other expert assistance is required, the services of a competent professional person should be sought.

From a Declaration of Principles Jointly Adopted by a Committee of the American Bar Association and a Committee of Publishers and Associations

ISBN: 1-59546-243-0

This product is not intended to provide legal or financial advice or substitute for the advice of an attorney or advisor.

Printing number 10 9 8 7 6 5 4 3 2 1

Building
A Successful
Business Plan:
Advice from the Experts

Special acknowledgment to the following:

Tracy Butzko, Managing Editor; Steve Pincich, Editor; Chip Butzko, Encouragement Press, Production; Jeannie Staats, Product Manager; Derek Vander Laan, Cover Art; Peri Hughes, Editor; Alison Somilleda, Copy Editor; Kristen Grant, Production Associate; Edgewater Editorial Services, Inc.

The Editors of Socrates extend a special thanks to the following business leaders to contributed to the content of this book:

William A. Lederer, Elizabeth Milnikel, Kelly Mizeur, Sara Shifin and Patrick J. Spain.

Get the most out of
Building A Successful Business Plan.

Get the most out of Building a Successful Business Plan: Advice from the Experts. Take advantage of the enclosed CD and special access to Building a Successful Business Plan: Advice from the Experts resource section of Socrates.com that are included with this purchase.

The CD and Buidling a Successful Business Plan resource section offer readers a unique opportunity both to build on the material contained in the book and to utilize tools such as forms, checklists, spreadsheets and appraisals that will save time and money. More than $100 worth of free forms and content are provided.

The CD bound into the back cover contains a read-only version of this book. Readers can access the dedicated Business Plan resource section by registering their purchase at Socrates.com. A special eight-digit Registration Code is provided on the CD. Once registered, a variety of free forms, checklists, appraisals, research articles, government forms and other useful tools are available at

www.socrates.com/books/business-plan.aspx

From time to time, new material will be added and readers will be informed of changes in the law, as well as updates to the content of this book.

Finally, readers are offered discounts on selected Socrates products designed to help implement and manage their business and personal matters more efficiently.

Table of Contents

CD

Appendix A: Sample Business Plans

Appendix B: Bios of Contributing Business Leaders

Section ■ One

1 Why Write a Business Plan?

Overview

Starting and growing a business takes motivation and talent. It also takes research and planning. Although initial mistakes are not always fatal, it takes extra skill, discipline and hard work to regain the advantage. Take time beforehand to explore and evaluate your business and personal goals, then use this information to build a comprehensive and thoughtful business plan that will help you reach these goals.

Developing a business plan will force you to think through some important issues that you may not otherwise consider. Your plan will become a valuable tool as you set out to raise money for your business. Are you ready to expand your business to the next level and need additional financing to help get you there? Have you reached capacity at your current location and need a larger space to increase capacity? Have you identified a void in a growing market and want to fill that void with a new product or service?

A business plan presents the roadmap you need to help you reach your goals. It is not just for planning your business. It also provides you with milestones to gauge your success. Through every venture in life, you need a roadmap. Your business plan is your roadmap. It keeps you focused and guides you to your desired destination. It is a vital sales tool to obtain financing and provides investors a necessary look at the details of your business.

> "That business is you—everything you say, everything you do or do not do. Everybody reads off of your set of values that they take as the guiding principles of what is appropriate. I have learned over the years that signaling is really important. Oftentimes it is not what you say, but what you do."
>
> **William Lederer**
> **Chairman & CEO**
> **Minotaur Capital**
> **Management**
> **Chicago, IL**

> ## A complete business plan will cover all aspects of your business:
> - an examination of the product or service (your purpose)
> - the market (customers)
> - the industry (competitors)
> - marketing and sales (distribution and pricing)
> - production (costs and the process)
> - management (people)
> - financing (equity/debt structure)

Your plan outlines each activity in detail to include timing and constraints.

Are You Ready to Own a Business?

Is Entrepreneurship for You?

In business, there are no guarantees. There is simply no way to eliminate all the risks associated with starting a small business, but you can improve your chances of success with good planning, preparation and insight. Start by evaluating your strengths and weaknesses as a potential owner and manager of a small business. Carefully consider each of the following questions:

- Are you a self-starter? It will be entirely up to you to develop projects, organize your time and follow through on details.

- How well do you get along with different personalities? Business owners need to develop working relationships with a variety of people including customers, vendors, staff, bankers and professionals such as lawyers, accountants or consultants. Can you deal with a demanding client, an unreliable vendor or a cranky receptionist if your business interests demand it?

- How good are you at making decisions? Small business owners are required to make decisions constantly—often quickly, independently and under pressure.

- Do you have the physical and emotional stamina to run a business? Business ownership can be exciting, but it is also a lot of work. Can you face six or seven 12-hour workdays every week?

- How well do you plan and organize? Research indicates that poor planning is responsible for most business failures. Good organization—of financials, inventory, schedules and production—can help you avoid many pitfalls.

- Is your drive strong enough? Running a business can wear you down emotionally. Some business owners burn out quickly from having to carry all the responsibility for the success of their business on their own shoulders. Strong motivation will help you survive slowdowns and periods of burnout.

- How will the business affect your family? The first few years of business startup can be hard on family life. It is important for family members to know what to expect and for you to be able to trust that they will support you during this time. There also may be financial difficulties until the business becomes profitable, which could take months or years. You may have to adjust to a lower standard of living or put family assets at risk in the short term.

- What are your goals? What are your goals for your business? Maybe you want to create a small business that remains small and provides you with a steady income. Or your goal may be to start a business with the plan to sell it once it becomes successful. Your goals will determine the type of business to start, how much time and money you want to invest to make it a success and what you want to take out of your business.

Do You Have What It Takes?

What does it take to be an entrepreneur? Which personality traits make for success? Some people think that to be an entrepreneur you must be born that way. In truth, anyone can learn to operate like an entrepreneur.

What are the similarities of successful entrepreneurs?

• persistence	• high energy level	• inquisitiveness
• ability to consolidate resources	• desire for immediate feedback	• willingness to be an agent of change
• strong drive to achieve	• demanding nature	• goal-oriented behavior
• independence	• creativity	• self-confidence
• commitment	• strong integrity	• innovation
• vision	• calculated risk taking	• problem-solving skills
• competitiveness	• tolerance for ambiguity	• high reliability
• luck	• desire to work hard	• strong management and organizational skills
• personal initiative	• tolerance for failure	

"Being a successful entrepreneur requires the right mix of focus and flexibility. You need need to stay focused on the ultimate goal. At the same time, you need to execute flexibly, changing your approach and challenging your preconceptions in response to what you discover as you develop your business."

Patrick J. Spain
CEO, HighBeam Research, Inc.
Co-Founder and former CEO, Hoover's, Inc.

> **Remember**
>
> - Look for new ideas.
> - Keep it simple.
> - If at first you don't succeed…try and try again.

"It is possible to spend too much time on developing a business plan. Building a business plan should be done in a great flurry of activity and with great intensity. You build it and you move on, revisiting it regularly, but not more so."

William Lederer, Chairman & CEO
Minotaur Capital Management
Chicago, IL

Self-Evaluation Exercises

You need to think about why you would like to own your own business. What makes you think you will be successful in business? Carefully consider each of the following questions. They deal with the basic personality of potential entrepreneurs.

- Are you entrepreneurial enough to build a business?
- Do you know the meaning of the word Entrepreneurial?
- Are you a risk-taker?
- Did you get good grades in school? (Many successful entrepreneurs did not.)
- If you are a cautious person and a good student, should you forget the whole thing? (Some entrepreneurial tests suggest so.)

There are many successful business owners who, as adolescents, were team players, athletes, school leaders or excellent students and never seriously questioned the status quo. Often, though, a tendency toward caution is not typical of successful entrepreneurs. They tend to be maverick personalities with risk-taking vision and courage. Many tend to be just a bit offbeat, and they sometimes need to be in order to creatively grow a successful business.

Obviously, there is no set formula for success. However, we have created an entrepreneurial test that may help you in your personal evaluation process. You just need to remember that this is simply a tool. It is fun to take and fun to interpret, but you should keep it in perspective.

Think Strategically

To be effective as a leader, you must develop skills in strategic thinking. Strategic thinking is a process in which you learn how to make your business vision a reality by developing your abilities in teamwork, problem solving and critical thinking. It is also a tool to help you confront change, plan for and make transitions, and envision new possibilities and opportunities. It is a critical management skill

Strategic thinking requires you to envision what you want your ideal outcome to be for your business and then work backward by focusing on the story of how you will be able to reach your vision.

As you develop a strategic vision for your business, there are five different criteria that you should focus on. These five criteria will help you define your ideal outcome. In addition, each skill will help you set up and develop the steps necessary to make your business vision a reality.

The five criteria of the strategic thinking process include:

1. Organization

The organization of your business involves the people you will have working for you, the organizational structure of your business and the resources necessary to make it all work. What will your organization look like? What type of structure will support your vision? How will you combine people, resources and structure together to achieve your ideal outcome?

2. Observation

When you are looking down at the world from an airplane, you can see much more than when you are on the ground—you see the big picture. Strategic thinking is much the same in that it allows you to see things from higher up. By increasing your powers of observation, you will begin to become more aware of what motivates people, how to solve problems more effectively and how to distinguish between alternatives.

3. Views

Views are simply different ways of thinking about something. In strategic thinking, there are four viewpoints to take into consideration when forming your business strategy: the environmental view; the marketplace view; the project view; and the measurement view. Views can be used as tools to help you think about outcomes, identify critical elements and adjust your actions to achieve your ideal position.

4. Driving Forces

What are the driving forces that will make your ideal outcome a reality? What is your company's vision and mission? Driving forces usually lay the foundation for what you want people to focus on in your business (i.e., what you will use to motivate others to perform). Examples of driving forces might include: individual and organizational incentives; empowerment and alignment; qualitative factors such as a defined vision, values and goals; productive factors like a mission or function; quantitative factors such as results or experience; and others such as commitment, coherent action, effectiveness, productivity and value.

5. Ideal Position

After working through the first four phases of the strategic thinking process, you should be able to define your ideal position. Your ideal position outline should include:

- the conditions you have found to be necessary if your business is to be productive;
- the niche in the marketplace that your business will fill;
- any opportunities that may exist either currently or in the future for your business;
- the core competencies or skills required in your business; and
- the strategies and tactics you will use to pull it all together.

By working through these five areas, you will begin to get a clearer picture of exactly how your business vision can be accomplished. As your vision becomes more focused, your ideas will appear stronger and more credible. Not only will it be easier to convince others that your idea is a good one, but it will also be easier to maintain your own conviction and motivation when you reach any pitfalls or obstacles in the road.

Overall, you can apply strategic thinking skills to any area of your life. But by making a concerted effort to apply them specifically to your business venture, you will have a much better chance of bringing your vision to life.

Know Thyself

Not everyone is cut out to be an entrepreneur. It takes a special talent. Some owners of small businesses have it and some do not. Before you invest time, energy, money and a piece of your heart, it is important to do some serious self-analysis to answer such questions as:

> "Why did I become an entrepreneur? Because I discovered that my streak of independence and lack of respect for established norms, made me functionally unemployable in the corporate world. And I still had to make a living."
>
> **Patrick J. Spain, CEO HighBeam Research, Inc. Co-Founder and former CEO, Hoover's, Inc.**

- Am I prepared to work hard and make sacrifices?
- Am I self-disciplined?
- Do I have management ability?

- Am I experienced enough in this field?
- What do I want out of life?
- Are my goals realistic and attainable?

Studies have shown that entrepreneurs are persevering and not easily defeated. They thrive in a challenging environment and have a tremendous need to be in control. They turn diversity into opportunity. They are risk takers. They welcome responsibility, and they are willing and able to make decisions.

Moreover, successful entrepreneurs are patient and able to wait out the sometimes slow beginnings of a business. They also are able to learn from their mistakes, trust their own judgment and have an optimistic outlook.

> "The main thing is to be the kind of person who knows herself—someone who has an inner confidence; someone who is not just willing to take risks but understands what kinds of risks she is actually willing to take; someone who is willing to learn and accept the fact that she does not know everything and will seek out help; someone who is flexible. Too many people who work on a business plan already have envisioned what the business will look like and then intend to ignore any research that contradicts how they want their business to look."
>
> **Sara Shifrin**
> **Director of Entrepreneur Training**
> **Women's Business Development Center**
> **Chicago, IL**

What Makes an Entrepreneur?

- A willingness to take on acceptable risk. The really risk-averse people will not be the best entrepreneurs.

- Taking on a smart, measured amount of risk. People that may have done it before. People who have been given a lot of freedom in a corporate structure to launch a new product or take risks.

- They are not intimidated by sales. There are a lot of entrepreneurs who are not good at sales—and these people's businesses will not be as successful. If you cannot sell your product or services, it is going to be hard for you to hire or train someone to do it for you.

- Quickly identifying the things you want to be involved in or not involved in and getting someone in who will do the tasks you do not do. But you still need to understand every aspect if you are in charge.

Kelly Mizeur, Finance Counselor
Women's Business Development Center
Chicago, IL

Getting Started

Starting your own business is a lot more complicated than most people realize. Knowing what type of business to start is something else.

1. **List your reasons for wanting to go into business. Some of the most common reasons for starting a business are:**
   - self-management
   - financial independence
   - creative freedom
   - full use of personal skills and knowledge

2. **Next determine what business is right for you. Ask yourself these questions:**
   - What do I like to do with my time?
   - What technical skills have I learned or developed?
   - What do others say I am good at?
   - Will I have the support of my family?
   - How much time do I have to run a successful business?
   - Do I have any hobbies or interests that are marketable?

3. **Identify your business niche. Research and answer these questions:**
   - What business am I interested in starting?
   - What services or products will I sell?
   - Is my idea practical, and will it fill a need?
   - What is my competition?
   - What is my business's advantage over existing firms?
   - Can I deliver a better quality of service?
   - Can I create a demand for my business?

4. **The final step before developing your plan is the pre-business checklist. You should answer these questions:**
   - What skills and experience do I bring to the business?
   - What legal structure will I use?
   - How will my company's business records be maintained?
   - What insurance coverage will be needed?
   - What equipment or supplies will I need?
   - How will I compensate myself?
   - What are my resources?
   - What financing will I need?
   - Where will my business be located?
   - What will I name my business?

Your answers will help you create a focused, well-researched business plan that will serve as a blueprint for business operations, management and capitalization.

Once you have completed your business plan
associate. When you feel comfortable with t'
discuss it with your banker. The business p'
change as your business grows.

Buying a Business

Many find the idea of running a small '
motivation after dealing with business
with startups. For those disheartened'
existing business is often a simpler ;

Advantages

The main reason to buy an existing business is the u..
costs of time, money a..
addition, cash flow may start ın..
thanks to existing inventory and
receivables. Other benefits include pre-
existing customer goodwill and easier
financing opportunities if the business has
a positive track record.

**Startup Basics
Rules of Thumb:**

- **Everything will take longer
  than you expect.**

- **Everything will cost more.**

- **People will disappoint you.**

- **You will never have enough
  resources to do the quality
  of work that you want in the
  time that you think is needed.**

- **A revenue rule of thumb for
  most entrepreneurs (most
  small businesses) is time is
  not on your side. It is really
  important to drive revenue in
  these instances; you have to
  be disciplined about costs.**

**William Lederer
Chairman & CEO
Minotaur Capital Management
Chicago, IL**

Disadvantages

The biggest block to buying a small
business outright is the initial purchase
cost. Because the business concept,
customer base, brands and other
fundamental work has already been done,
the financial cost of acquiring an existing
business is usually greater than starting one
from nothing. Other possible disadvantages
include hidden problems associated with
the business and receivables that are valued
at the time of purchase but later turn out
to be noncollectable. Good research is the
key to avoiding these problems.

Buying a Franchise

An important step in the small business
startup process is deciding whether or not
to go into business at all. Each year, thousands of potential entrepreneurs are
faced with this difficult decision. Because of the risk and work involved in starting
a new business, many new entrepreneurs choose franchising as an alternative to
starting a new, independent business from scratch.

One of the biggest mistakes you can make is to hurry into business, so it is
important to understand your reasons for going into business and to determine if
owning a business is right for you.

If you are concerned about the risk involved in a new, independent business
venture, then franchising may be the best business option for you. But remember

rk, dedication and sacrifice are essential to the success of any enture, including franchising.

anchise is a legal and commercial relationship between the owner of a ademark, service mark, trade name or advertising symbol and an individual or group wishing to use that identification in a business. The franchise governs the method of conducting business between the two parties. Generally, a franchisee sells goods or services supplied by the Franchiser or that meet the Franchiser's quality standards.

Franchising is based on mutual trust between the Franchiser and franchisee. The Franchiser provides the business expertise (marketing plans, management guidance, financing assistance, site location, training, etc.) that otherwise would not be available to the franchisee. The franchisees bring to the franchise operation the entrepreneurial spirit and drive necessary to make the franchise a success.

There are primarily two forms of franchising:

1. **Product/trade name franchising**–In the simplest form, a Franchiser owns the right to the name or trademark and sells that right to a franchisee. This is known as product/trade name franchising.

2. **Business format franchising**–The more complex form, business format franchising, involves a broader ongoing relationship between the two parties. Business format franchises often provide a full range of services, including site selection, training, product supply, marketing plans, and even assistance in obtaining financing.

There are a number of advantages and disadvantages to owning a franchise. See Chapter 18.

For more information about franchising, use the "Buying a Franchise" book available at Socrates.com.

Learning the Language of Business

Readers are entitled to full access and use of the comprehensive Business Law and Accounting & Finance Dictionaries found on the Web landing page at www.socrates.com/books/business-plan.aspx. Please remember to register the first time you use this free resource. See page iv for instructions.

Pulling It All Together

1. List your goals for your business.

2. List your reasons for wanting to go into business.

3. Take the Are You an Entrepreneur? test. Do you have the traits to be an entrepreneur?

4. Describe your personal skills and experiences.

5. Determine which business is right for you.

6. Identify your business niche.

7. Identify your market.

8. Describe your startup plans.

9. Review your current finances:
    - list your assets
    - list your current cash flow
    - estimate your expenses
    - how will you compensate yourself?

10. What legal structure will you use?

11. How will your company's business records be maintained?

12. What insurance coverage will you need?

13. What equipment or supplies will you need?

14. What are your resources?

15. What financing will you need?

16. Where will your business be located?

17. What will you name your business?

Get your plan reviewed and review the reviewer's comments. Contact the local branch of your Small Business Administration or the Small Business Development Center to review it for you. Refer to Chapter 21 for an SBA center near you.

Free Forms and Checklists

Registered readers can visit www.socrates.com/books/business-plan.aspx for free forms, letters and checklists. To register, see page iv for details. Among the many items available are:

Simple Contract • Cash Flow Forecast • Break Even Analysis • Independent Contractor Agreement • Commercial Lease • Stock Certificate • Personal Financial Statement • And more!

2 Building a Business Plan– Executive Summary

Overview

Although it is the shortest section of your business plan, the executive summary is actually the most important component of your plan. It summarizes who you are, what your company does, where your company is going and how you are going to get there. You have less than 2 minutes to grab an investor's attention. Your summary must be thorough, compelling and entice the reader to read on. It is the most carefully read section of the entire document. Therefore, it must describe your company, product and market opportunities in a concise and engaging manner.

Although the summary appears in the front of your plan, write it after your plan is complete. Write up one paragraph to describe each section of the plan. Finish your summary by listing the amount of money required and the major advantages your company will have over the competition. This is also a good place to note that you have additional backup information.

> "The executive summary of the business plan is extremely important because it will break the ice and entice someone to want to look at the other parts of the business plan. It should be no longer than two pages—three at most. The hardest thing is to say what you have to say and stop saying it."
>
> **Sara Shifrin**
> **Director of**
> **Entrepreneur Training**
> **Women's Business**
> **Development Center**
> **Chicago, IL**

A well-written business plan will provide a snapshot of your vision, your plan and your goals. The hardest part of writing a business plan is just putting your ideas on paper. Do not be afraid to write your goals down. An important part of writing your plan is actually putting your ideas in writing.

The executive summary touches on all the important parts of your plan. Keep your summary short. It should be no longer than two pages and include detailed descriptions of:

Company Overview

The company overview describes the purpose of your business using your mission statement, values and vision statements.

> **Mission Statement:** State your company's mission or purpose. What is it your company will do?
>
> **Goals and Objectives:** List all the major goals you have set for your company, along with the objectives you want to meet to achieve your goals.
>
> **Values Statement:** This is the set of beliefs and principles that guide your company actions and decisions.
>
> **Vision Statement:** Where do you want to go and what do you want your company to become?

Business Environment

This section reviews your business environment. List any situations that may be out of your control such as the nature of your industry, the direction of the marketplace or the intensity of your competition. Analyze all opportunities and threats your company will face in the current environment, and what it will take to make your company successful.

Company Description

The company description identifies your company's specific capabilities and resources. Include a brief description of everything you bring to your industry that is unique—including your management team, company organization, any technology you will be utilizing or capitalizing upon, products and services, company operations and marketing potential.

Company Strategy

Map out your basic strategies for your business using all the information you have learned about your industry, competition and markets. Explain how the strategy you have picked is the right one for your business. Outline what your business needs to do to make your strategy succeed.

> **"One of the things I always look for in a business plan is that the narrative portion and financial statement section are understandable and realistic and that the two tie together."**
>
> **Curtis Roeschley**
> **Director**
> **Jane Addams Hull House Association**
> **Small Business Development Center**
> **Chicago, IL**

Financial Review

The financial review should include key financial documents to support your projections. It is critical that your financials and your narrative tie together. If they do not, you will be sending a big red flag to your investors. If your financials and narrative do not tie together, you are either too optimistic about your sales or do not understand the numbers. Avoid sending mixed signals to investors and potentially losing an investor's interest. Carefully create and describe your financial projections by using several standard financial statements. Then back it up with your narrative. While these statements are merely estimates, they will provide a glimpse of where you stand today and where you expect to be in the future.

> **Income Statement:** Create a summary of revenues your company brings in over a month, a quarter or a year. Then subtract the total costs involved in running your business during that same time period. The net revenue is your bottom line showing the profit that you made during that period.
>
> **Balance Sheet**: This is a reference of your financial condition at any particular moment. The balance sheet shows exactly what your company owns, what money it owes and revenues outstanding to produce a picture of what your company is worth. See Chapter 20: Planning Worksheets for a "Sample Balance Sheet."
>
> **Cash-Flow Statement:** A cash-flow statement traces the flow of cash in and out of your company during any given period. The cash-flow statement only tracks money when you actually receive it or spend it. See Chapter 20: Planning Worksheets for a "Sample Cash-Flow Statement."

Action Plan

Provide details about your action plan— actions you plan to take to carry out your business plan. In this section, point out proposed changes in management or in the organization, including new policies, procedures and skills you will need to put the plan to work.

Pulling It All Together

The executive summary is the most carefully read section of your business plan. Write a clear, concise executive summary that is informative, engaging and entertaining. Use this outline to create your executive summary.

> "My advice to all entrepreneurs for creating a business plan is to map backward from the future to the present. Imagine all the steps necessary to achieve that success, then ask yourself, 'What will be the permutations and combinations along the way? How do I systematically try to reduce the risk of not making my goals?' Answer these questions and you will be prepared for the inevitable bumps in the road. "
>
> **William Lederer**
> **Chairman & CEO**
> **Minotaur Capital Management**
> **Chicago, IL**

Company Overview

Describe the purpose of your business. Include the following information:

Mission Statement

1. Describe your company's mission or purpose.
2. What is it your company will do? (Describe the products or services you will be offering.)

Goals and Objectives

1. List all the major goals you have set for your company.

2. List all objectives you want to meet to achieve your goals.

Values Statement

1. State the beliefs and principles that guide your company actions and decisions.

Vision Statement

1. Describe where you want your company to be in 3 to 5 years.

2. Where do you want to go and what do you want your company to become?

Business Environment

1. List any situations that may be out of your control such as the nature of your industry, the direction of the marketplace or the intensity of your competition.

2. Analyze all opportunities, the threats your company will face in the current environment and what it will take to make your company successful.

Company Description

Include a brief description of everything you bring to your industry that is unique:

- your management team
- company organization
- any technology you will be utilizing or capitalizing upon
- your products and services
- company operations
- marketing potential

Company Strategy

1. Map out your basic strategies for your business using all the information you have learned about your industry, competition and markets.

2. Explain how the strategy you have picked is the right one for your business.

3. Outline what your business needs to do to make your strategy succeed.

Financial Review

1. Income Statement

2. Balance Sheet

3. Cash-Flow Statement

Action Plan

1. List the actions you plan to take to carry out your business plan.

2. Point out proposed changes in management or in the organization, including new policies, procedures and skills you will need to put the plan to work.

3 What Is Going on in the Industry

Overview

Knowing and really understanding your markets, your industry and your audience is usually the weakest part of any business plan. Most of us think we know all about our competition, changing industry trends and shifts in the marketplace and are completely surprised when we learn we do not know as much as we thought we did. Staying aware of changes in the industry, competitors and their product and service offerings, and changes in consumer wants and needs is directly tied to the success of a business. Thoroughly analyzing trends, needs and statistics will keep your business in tune with changing markets, enabling you to proactively plan and, if necessary, react quickly.

Hint
An industry is a group of related businesses.

Structure

Every industry has its own shape and structure. The number of competitors has a major impact on the shape of an industry. To understand the structure of your industry you will need to know as much as possible about:

- competition
- entry barriers
- new technology
- exit barriers

Industry Analysis

Industry analysis assesses:

- general industry environment in which you compete
- industry trends and statistics

Competition

An industry is not necessarily made up of many different companies; an industry may be a monopoly of only one company if it does not have any competitors, or it may be a small number of strong competitors, or even a group of viable competitors. To understand your competition, make a list of all major competitors in your industry, then answer the questionnaire on the next page.

"Every company has competition. Often new business owners think they do not have any competition. If they do not think they have any competition, that is a red flag. Even if there is not a direct competitor there is always a potential consumer in their field or a related industry making a buying decision about a product or service that will affect the new business and have an impact on its sales. So it is important to identify direct and indirect competitors, and to determine the specific niche that you are going to provide. Know how to distinguish your business in the market and how you will compete, tapping an unmet need and looking for ways to offer such things as better quality, a cheaper price or a more comprehensive service."

Curtis Roeschley
Director
Jane Addams Hull House
Association—Small Business
Development Center
Chicago, IL

Technology

Changing technology is a major driver of many industries. How much of technology is driving your business, and how fast is it changing? Who is controlling the technologies that affect your industry, and how easily can the technologies be obtained?

Entry Barriers

Entry barriers are the obstacles that make it difficult for new competitors to enter a market. Some barriers are predictable such as high capital costs that require a lot of money up front or a complex distribution system that makes it hard to reach customers. Other entry barriers are easy to overlook. Economies of scale—in which the bigger you are, the more money you will make—often discourage brand new competitors. Strong customer loyalty or the high cost of changing products can also create barriers for new players in the field.

Exit Barriers

How difficult is it for companies in an industry to get out of the market if they want to? The ties and attachments that keep competitors around are called exit barriers. Exit barriers can include everything from expensive factories or specialized equipment that cannot be sold easily to long-term labor contracts, customer warranties, leases or service agreements and government regulations.

How much do you really know about your industry? Answer these questions to determine your level of knowledge.

Industry Analysis Questionnaire				
The number of competitors in your industry is:	Many	Some	Few	Unknown
Your industry is dominated by several large firms:	Yes	No		Unknown
The combined market share of the three largest companies in your industry is:	<40%	40-80%	>80%	Unknown
New technologies change the way your industry does business every:	Year	5 years	10 years	Unknown
The barriers that stop new competitors from entering your industry are:	High	Medium	Low	Unknown
Overall market demand in your industry is:	Growing	Stable	Declining	Unknown
There is a large, untapped market that your industry can take advantage of:	Yes	Maybe	No	Unknown
Your industry offers a selection of features and options in its product line that is:	Extensive	Average	Limited	Unknown
Customers buy products in your industry based almost entirely on price:	Yes	No		Unknown
Customers can find other alternatives to take the place of your industry's products:	Easily	With difficulty	No	Unknown
Suppliers to your industry have a lot of influence when it comes to setting terms:	Yes	No		Unknown
Customers have a lot of bargaining power when buying your industry's products:	Yes	No		Unknown
Distributors have a lot of power and play a major role in your industry:	Yes	No		Unknown
Overall costs in your industry have been:	Rising	Stable	Declining	Unknown
Profit margins in your industry are:	Strong	Average	Weak	Unknown

Your answers should give you an idea of how much you know about your industry. Any box checked unknown indicates that you need to take a closer look and find out more.

Product Choices

Conduct a quick survey of the similarities and differences between products and services in your market. The difference is called product differentiation. If each product looks a lot like the next, then price may be the only differentiation and will become more important to the customer than product features. If each product is different and offers the customer something unique, then product features are likely to determine long-term success or failure in the market.

Substitutes

Suddenly, a completely new type of product or service, usually from another industry or new technology, threatens to become a rival to your product or service and erode your market share. For example, digital cameras and cell phone cameras threaten still photography; e-mail and instant messaging challenge traditional phone service. This is called product substitution—when new products take over existing ones in fast-changing, highly competitive markets.

Relationships

Business is all about relationships. It is not what you know, but who you know. Building strong relationships with your suppliers and distributors is just as important as building good relations with your customers.

Suppliers

Your relationship with suppliers drives the entire structure of your business. Every company relies on outside suppliers at some stage of the process, whether for basic supplies and raw material or for the entire finished product or service. When outside suppliers are introduced into the equation, the availability, complexity and importance of your product and service is controlled by the type of relationship you have cultivated with the supplier. That includes price, credit terms, delivery schedules, etc.

Are there any suppliers that may limit your ability to provide a product or service to your customers? Are there any suppliers you can enter into a long-term agreement with to reduce costs and pass the savings along to the consumer? How do you protect yourself if a supplier turns into a competitor?

Good Customer Relations

Customers have the power to influence your business. As an industry becomes more competitive, the balance of power shifts toward the customer. A growing number of products and services provide the customer with more options. Demanding customers will often place pressure on companies to lower prices, expand service and develop new product features. To keep price from becoming a purchasing determinant, think of other ways in which you can compete without cutting into your profit margins.

Distributors

How you distribute your product or service and how long it takes to get it from producer to consumer will affect delivery price and terms. The selection of your products distribution channel determines the cost and length of time it takes to reach the customer. The longer the chain, the less control you will have over pricing and terms. The companies controlling the distribution of a product at the end of the chain have the greatest control because they have direct access to the customer.

Finance

Knowing the costs of doing business determines your profit level. What are your costs of doing business? What is your potential profit? Are costs increasing or is the cost of the product or service decreasing? The answer to these questions determines your profit level.

> **"Look at financial ratios to understand profit levels. You need to know what your industry average is so you are informed and not disillusioned as you create your business plan."**
>
> **Sara Shifrin**
> **Director of Entrepreneur Training**
> **Women's Business Development Center**
> **Chicago, IL**

Cost Trends

Separate your business into its various components. Where are the bulk of costs occurring in your company? What are your fixed and variable costs? Will you gain any economies of scale by purchasing in quantity? What happens if you sell twice the product or service? Will you make more profit? Try to pinpoint where you can lower fixed and variable costs.

Profit Margins

Industries have their own rules of thumb when it comes to expected profit margins—how much money they expect to end up with after all costs have been added is divided by the money collected. Changing profit margins in other industries often reflect changing capacity levels or how much a product or service in an industry can actually produce and deliver and will provide insight into the direction an industry is headed.

Markets

Customers create markets; and the number of customers determines the competition. The customers you are targeting represent the market that is ideal for your goods or services.

Market Size

The size of the market can tell you a lot about what is likely to happen to it over time. Large markets attract competitors while smaller markets are easily overlooked but may present more favorable business opportunities. You can capitalize on niche markets (finding a new use for your product or service that no one else has thought of before).

Market Growth

A growing market offers the best odds for new companies to gain market share from existing competition.

A shrinking market will force established competitors to become leaner and more efficient. As markets change in size in either direction, the competition will most likely heat up.

Sources of Industry Information

Collecting industry information can be a time-consuming and overwhelming task. Often the information is not available or is difficult to find. Here are a few places you can check to learn more about an industry:

Government Sources

U.S. government agencies have already done most of the data collection work for you, and most information is free of charge. Check out the Securities and Exchange Commission to view quarterly filing reports for public companies as well as the Department of Commerce, the Federal Trade Commission, the Justice Department and other regulatory agencies. Visit your state government Web site to view specific state statistics and check with the Better Business Bureau.

> "When you are doing the sales projections, your best source of information is your competition or a trade association in your industry, or talk to a shop owner next to where you want to be located, or someone who runs your same exact business but they are going after business in [a] different part of the country."
>
> **Kelly Mizeur**
> **Finance Counselor**
> **Women's Business**
> **Development Center**
> **Chicago, IL**

The American Community Survey (ACS) is a new nationwide survey designed by the Census Bureau to provide annual economic, social and housing information traditionally collected by the decennial census long form. The ACS will collect information on subjects such as age, gender, race, family composition, industry and occupation, income and poverty, education, employment, commuting patterns, and housing that will be used to develop census-like profiles. It will replace the long form in future censuses and is a critical element in the Census Bureau's re-engineered 2010 census plan.

The ACS is a large monthly household survey conducted using mailed questionnaires, telephone interviews and visits from the Census Bureau's field representatives. It produces annual and multiyear averages of population and housing characteristics for small geographic and population groups. The ACS will provide new social, economic and housing profiles every year for all states, cities, counties, metropolitan areas or population groups of 65,000 or more people.

The ACS will provide census-type profiles every year. It will not, however, provide a count of the population. The Census Bureau will still conduct the decennial census to count the population and will continue the intercensal program of population estimates.

View a sample ACS Statistics profile in Chapter 20: Planning Worksheets.

Trade Associations

Many industries are supported by trade groups that keep track of what is going on within a region and the world. Local organizations such as a chamber of commerce can be very useful in providing information.

Libraries

Public libraries house a number of business periodicals, references, industry newsletters and annual reports of large corporations, as do business and university libraries.

Pulling It All Together

Understanding industry trends and directions is key to building a successful business plan. Knowing the demographics and universe of your market enables you to build targeted marketing and sales plans. Keeping track of impact factors, obstacles, opportunities and threats allows you to forecast and build strategies and plan for the future. Use this outline to analyze your industry, understand your markets and become aware of obstacles, opportunities and threats.

I. Industry Description

Describe your industry.

II. Industry Analysis

Refer to your answers in the industry analysis questionnaire mentioned earlier in this chapter. Include commentary to each of the questions you answered:

1. The number of competitors in your industry is:

2. Your industry is dominated by several large firms:

3. The combined market share of the three largest companies in your industry is:

4. New technologies change the way your industry does business every:

5. The barriers that stop new competitors from entering your industry are:

6. Overall market demand in your industry is:

7. There's a large, untapped market that your industry can take advantage of:

8. Your industry offers a selection of features and options in its product line that is:

9. Customers buy products in your industry based entirely on price:

10. Customers can find other alternatives to take the place of your industry's products:

11. Suppliers to your industry have a lot off influence when it comes to setting terms:

12. Customers have significant bargaining power when buying your industry's products

13. Distributors have a lot of power and play a major role in your industry:

14. Overall costs in your industry have been:

15. Profit margins in your industry are:

Provide a brief overview of your questionnaire findings in your industry analysis summary.

III. Competition

1. Make a list of all major competitors in your industry.

2. Divide the list into primary, secondary and tertiary competitors.

IV. New Technology

1. List all new technology that is available and how it will affect your business.

2. Summarize how much of technology is driving your business and how fast it is changing.

3. Describe who is controlling the technologies that affect your industry and how easily can the technologies be obtained?

V. Entry Barriers

1. List all entry barriers you have identified that will make it difficult to enter a market.

2. Describe how you plan to overcome these barriers.

VI. Exit Barriers

1. List any exit barriers that will prevent you from exiting a market if you decide to discontinue a product or service.

VII. Product Choices

1. Conduct a quick survey of the similarities and differences between products and services in your market.

2. Summarize the differences.

VIII. Relationships

1. Describe your relationship with suppliers and distributors including terms, pricing, discounts and delivery schedules.

2. Note if there are any suppliers that may limit your ability to provide a product or service to your customers.

3. List the suppliers with whom you can enter into a long-term agreement to reduce costs, and pass the savings along to the consumer.

4. Describe how you will be able to protect yourself if a supplier turns into a competitor.

IX. Good Customer Relations

1. To keep price from becoming a purchasing determinant, list the other ways you can compete without cutting into your profit margins.

X. Finance

1. Calculate your unit sale price and expenses to determine your costs of doing business. (Use worksheet.)

2. What is your potential profit by unit, month, quarter or year?

3. Are costs increasing or is the cost of the product or service decreasing?

XI. Cost Trends

1. Identify where the bulk of costs are occurring in your company.

2. Determine your fixed and variable costs.

3. Will you gain any economies of scale by purchasing in quantity?

4. What happens if you sell twice the product or service? Will you make more profit?

5. Pinpoint where you can lower fixed and variable costs.

XII. Profit Margins

1. What is the standard profit margin reported for your industry?

2. How does your profit margin compare to industry standards?

XIII. Market Size

1. State the size (or total universe) of your primary market. Identify your source.

2. List any niche markets that you believe will have a use for your product or service. Indicate the size or universe of the niche.

3. Describe the reasons why you think the niche market will find your product or service useful.

XIV. Market Growth

1. Is your market growing or shrinking?

2. Is the number of competitors increasing or decreasing?

3. Is the total available number of buyers increasing or decreasing?

XV. Industry Opportunities and Threats

1. Identify any new opportunities available to your business. (Example: sudden spurts in market growth, new customer categories, improved technology, etc.)

XVI. Industry Threats

1. Identify any threats that may harm your business. (Example: economic slowdowns, changing trends, labor agreements, government regulations, etc.)

Section Two

4 Uniquely Yours— Company & Product/Service Description

Overview

Knowing your product or service offering inside and out is a success factor for your business plan. Highlighting features, benefits and product abilities will form the basis of your marketing strategy. Investors will examine your product and service descriptions closely to identify strengths and weaknesses in your overall business plan. If your description provides a complete and enthusiastic overview of your ideas, you will have a better chance of attracting investors. The following guidelines will help you assemble your company, product and service information and organize it into an exciting and convincing package.

Business Description

Start with a broad overview of the nature of your business. Describe why the company was formed, the nature and uniqueness of your products and services, and the general history and future goals of the company. Next, state your company's mission, including your goals and your future position within the industry. Then describe your company's business model and why it is unique to the industry.

Your business description needs to be clear, concise and visual. Describe your business by answering these questions:

1. Why are you going to be profitable?

2. Why will you succeed?

3. What direct experience does your management team have? If not direct, how relevant will their experience be to your business or industry? What do they offer to the business?

4. Have you talked with prospective or current customers? What are their comments?

5. Have you talked with competitors?

6. Is your business a quantity or quality business? At what volumes will you break even? Make a profit? Lose money?

7. Has your product or service matured within the industry?

8. How many industry turns do you expect every 6 months? Every 12 months?

9. What is the shelf life of your product?

10. When do you plan to open your doors for business?

11. Is your business seasonal in nature, with peaks and valleys in selling cycles, or will you have continuous selling year-round?

12. What are the days or hours you will be open? Will you be open nights, weekends or holidays? Why were these hours of operation chosen? Will you offer flexible or summer hours to employees?

13. How critical is your business location to customers or principal suppliers?

Product and Service Description

In this section you will be describing your products and services. Keep your descriptions short but vivid, painting a clear picture of your offering. Investors will buy into your plan faster if they are able to picture exactly what you are proposing. Follow this outline to paint a clear picture of your product or service.

Describe the uniqueness of your business in layperson's terms.

I. Describe the product, including physical characteristics, weight, size, color, packaging, etc.

II. Provide a detailed description of the manufacturing process of the product. Give a timeline that identifies the various stages of research, development and production.

III. Have you set up suppliers or distributors? Will they give you assistance?

IV. What credit terms are you going to make?

V. Describe your services. If you offer more than one service, outline each service in detail.

VI. What does your service deliver?

VII. What is the primary application of your service? What is the secondary application?

VIII. What need does your product or service fill?

IX. Who are your customers?

X. Who makes the buying decisions? If the buyer and the user are different, what is the relationship between them?

XI. What are the customer benefits?

XII. What makes it different?

XIII. Emphasize the uniqueness of your products/services.

XIV. State advantages and disadvantages of the product/service.

XV. State strengths/weaknesses of the product/service.

XVI. How difficult or easy is the product to use from a user's standpoint?

XVII. What are the results from using it?

XVIII. Why will a customer buy it?

XIX. What types of regulations are relevant and affect the production, sales or use of the product?

XX. Is training needed to use it? To sell it? Describe the training needed and how you provide the training.

XXI. Do you have any patents, trademarks, copyrights, etc.?

XXII. What ancillary products are available with the product/service?

XXIII. What stage of development are you in with your product/service?

XXIV. What is the price sensitivity?

XXV. How will the product be manufactured?

XXVI. What is your unique selling point?

XXVII. What is your product's/service's life cycle?

Outline Your Strategy

What is your company's strategy? Break it down into short-term and long-term objectives and how you intend to reach those objectives.

Key Elements investors look at when looking at a business plan are:
- **What problem are you solving, uniquely, persistently and deeply?**
- **How big is the problem?**
- **How persistent is the problem?**
- **Where is the problem?**
- **How will you accomplish solving this problem in terms of what you want to address, whether it is revenue, profitability, market penetration or where it becomes the ability to upsell or cross-sell other products or services?**
- **How large is the underlying, addressable market?**
- **Is the market relevant and is it being defined properly?**
- **What is the growth potential?**

William Lederer, Chairman & CEO
Minotaur Capital Management
Chicago, IL

The Business History and Your Experience

Tell the story of why you started your business. Every business was started for a reason—whether you saw a need in the marketplace that was not being fulfilled or you simply had a vision and felt compelled to follow it through. Why you started your company is important to staying the course.

> • Describe the status of your business—whether you are an existing business trying to attract investors to expand or you are starting a new company. State your targeted startup date or when you expect to secure funding.
>
> • Outline the legal structure of your company—where your company was founded, whether you are incorporated and the state in which you were incorporated. If you changed your incorporation status, show how and why your company status has changed.
>
> • Provide the names of all founding principals, stockholders and directors. If any changes have been made recently, mention all changes. If you have made any changes in the structure, management or ownership of the company, describe these changes in a brief and factual manner.
>
> • List any milestones and setbacks. Include a brief description of your lucky breaks or mild setbacks you may have suffered while starting the business. Describe how these occurrences have helped to form your current ideas or offerings.

Taste, Trends and Technology: How Will the Future Affect Your Business?

Following industry trends enables you to be flexible and adaptable. How will future trends affect your business? Has there been a significant change in technology that may affect your product or service? Has technology enabled you to provide a product or service cheaper and faster, or has it increased competition and made it more difficult for you to compete?

Critical Risks and Opportunities

Define any potential risks and opportunities your company will face, both internally and externally. Potential risks may include changes in management or the loss of a key employee. Opportunities may present themselves in the form of growth or new product development.

SWOT Analysis

A SWOT analysis is an assessment of a firm's strengths, weaknesses, opportunities and threats and is often the first tool used for determining a company's viability.

Strengths and weaknesses should always be determined with respect to rivals and not to one's own history. Yet some small businesses only focus on current rivals and therefore miss imminent threats from the emergence of new rivals. Therefore, both existing and emerging competitors should be considered when conducting a SWOT analysis.

Conducting an analysis using the SWOT framework helps you to focus your activities on areas where you are strongest and your greatest opportunities lie.

How to Use the SWOT Tool

To carry out a SWOT analysis, answer the following questions. Where appropriate, use similar questions:

Your Company's Strengths

> • What advantages does your product/service have?
>
> • What does your company do well?
>
> • What relevant resources do you have access to?
>
> • What do other people see as your company's strengths?

Consider your strengths from your own point of view and from the point of view of the people you deal with. Do not be modest. Be realistic and above all be honest with yourself.

In looking at your strengths, think about them in relation to your competitors. For example, if all your competitors provide high-quality products, then a high-quality production process is not a strength in the market, it is a necessity.

Your Company's Weaknesses

> • What could you improve?
>
> • What do you do badly?
>
> • What should you avoid?

Again, consider this from an internal and external basis: Do other people seem to perceive weaknesses that you do not see? Are your competitors doing better than you? It is best to be realistic now and face any unpleasant truths as soon as possible.

Available Opportunities

> Where are the good opportunities facing you?
>
> What are the interesting trends you are aware of?
>
> Useful opportunities can come from such things as:
>
> > • changes in technology and markets that may affect your business;
> >
> > • changes in government policy related to your field; or
> >
> > • changes in social patterns, population profiles, lifestyle changes, etc.

A useful approach to looking at opportunities is to look at your strengths and ask yourself whether these present any opportunities. Alternatively, look at your weaknesses and ask yourself whether you could open up opportunities by eliminating them.

Threats

> - What obstacles do you face?
> - What is your competition doing?
> - Are the required specifications for your job, products or services changing?
> - Is changing technology threatening your position?
> - Do you have bad debt or cash flow problems?
> - Could any of your weaknesses seriously threaten your business?

Carrying out this analysis will often be illuminating—both in terms of pointing out what needs to be done and in putting problems into perspective.

You can also apply SWOT analysis to your competitors. This may produce some interesting insights.

Example of a SWOT Analysis for a Small Consultancy Business

Strengths

> 1. We are able to respond very quickly as we have no red tape, no need for higher management approval, etc.
> 2. We are able to provide excellent customer care, as the current light workload means we have plenty of time to devote to customers.
> 3. Our lead consultant has a strong reputation within the market.
> 4. We can change direction quickly if we find that our marketing is not working or heading in the wrong direction.
> 5. We have little overhead, so we can offer good value to customers.

Weaknesses

> 1. Our company has no market presence or reputation.
> 2. We have a small staff with a shallow skills base in many areas.
> 3. We are vulnerable to vital staff being sick, leaving, etc.
> 4. Our cash flow will be unreliable in the early stages.

Opportunities

> 1. Our business sector is expanding, with many future opportunities for success.
> 2. Our local community promotes local businesses with work where possible.
> 3. Our competitors may be slow to adopt new technologies.

Threats

> 1. Future technological changes within our market may be greater than our ability to adapt to these changes.
>
> 2. A slight change in focus by a large competitor might wipe out any market position we achieve.
>
> 3. The consultancy, therefore, might decide to specialize in rapid response, good-value services to local businesses. Marketing would be placed in highly targeted local publications to get the greatest possible market presence for a set advertising budget. The consultancy should keep up-to-date with changes in technology where possible.

Key Points

SWOT analysis is a framework for analyzing your strengths and weaknesses and the opportunities and threats you face. This will help you to focus on your strengths, minimize weaknesses and take the greatest possible advantage of opportunities available. You should probably conduct a SWOT review of your business on a regular basis, depending on how fast your business environment, the industry and your own company changes.

Intellectual Property

Intellectual property refers to creations of the mind: inventions, literary and artistic works, and symbols, names, images and designs used in commerce.

Intellectual property is divided into two categories: industrial property, which includes inventions (patents), trademarks, industrial designs and geographic indications of source; and copyright, which includes literary such as novels, poems and plays, films, musical works and artistic works such as drawings, paintings, photographs and sculptures, and architectural designs. Rights related to copyright include those of performing artists in their performances, producers of phonograms in their recordings and those of broadcasters in their radio and television programs.

Patents, Trademarks, Service Marks and Copyrights

Some people confuse patents, copyrights and trademarks. Although there may be some similarities among these kinds of intellectual property protection, they are different and serve different purposes.

Patents

A patent for an invention is the grant of a property right to the inventor issued by the United States Patent and Trademark Office (USPTO). Generally, the term of a new patent is 20 years from the date on which the application for the patent was filed in the United States or, in special cases, from the date an earlier related application was filed, subject to the payment of maintenance fees. U.S. patent grants are effective only within the United States, U.S. territories and U.S. possessions. Under certain circumstances, patent term extensions or adjustments may be available.

Getting a patient is a lengthy, involved and expensive process that requires the application to prove the invention is truly different than anything known in the industry.

The right conferred by the patent grant is, in the language of the statute and of the grant itself, "the right to exclude others from making, using, offering for sale or selling" the invention in the United States or importing the invention into the United States. What is granted is not the right to make, use, offer for sale, sell or import, but the right to exclude others from making, using, offering for sale, selling or importing the invention. Once a patent is issued, the patentee must enforce the patent without aid of the USPTO.

There Are Three Types of Patents:

1. Utility patents may be granted to anyone who invents or discovers any new and useful process, machine, article of manufacture, or compositions of matters, or any new useful improvement thereof.

2. Design patents may be granted to anyone who invents a new, original and ornamental design for an article of manufacture.

3. Plant patents may be granted to anyone who invents or discovers and asexually reproduces any distinct and new variety of plants.

Trademarks and Service Marks

A Trademark is a word, name, symbol or device that is used in trade with goods to indicate the source of the goods and to distinguish them from the goods of others. A Service Mark is the same as a trademark except that it identifies and distinguishes the source of a service rather than a product. The terms trademark and mark are commonly used to refer to both trademarks and service marks.

Trademark rights may be used to prevent others from using a confusingly similar mark, but not to prevent others from making the same goods or from selling the same goods or services under a clearly different mark. Trademarks that are used in interstate or foreign commerce may be registered with the USPTO. Trademark protection is also available through state registries or the courts.

Copyrights

Copyright is a form of protection provided to the authors of original works of authorship including literary, dramatic, musical, artistic and certain other intellectual works, both published and unpublished. The 1976 Copyright Act generally gives the owner of copyright the exclusive right to reproduce the copyrighted work, to prepare derivative works, to distribute copies or phonorecords of the copyrighted work, to perform the copyrighted work publicly, or to display the copyrighted work publicly.

The copyright protects the form of expression rather than the subject matter of the writing. For example, a description of a machine could be copyrighted, but this would only prevent others from copying the description; it would not prevent others from writing a description of their own or from making and using the machine. Copyrights are registered by the Copyright Office of the Library of Congress, but some protection is available from the moment of creation.

General Information and Correspondence

If you have a question about a search, filing or general inquiries:

By Phone

800.786.9199 (in the United States or Canada) or 703.308.4357 for assistance from Customer Service Representatives and/or access to the automated information message system. Fax: 571.273.3245. TTY customers can dial 703.305.7785 for customer assistance.

By E-mail

usptoinfo@uspto.gov

By Mail

U.S. Patent and Trademark Office
Mail Stop USPTO Contact Center
P.O. Box 1450
Alexandria, VA 22313-1450

Correspondents should be sure to include their full return addresses, including zip codes. The principal location of the USPTO is Crystal Plaza 3, 2021 Jefferson Davis Highway, Arlington, Virginia.

The personal presence of applicants at the USPTO is unnecessary. You may conduct a search and file an application online at www.uspto.gov.

Visit www.uspto.gov/web/offices/ac/ido/oeip/catalog/index.html to view a catalog price list.

Pulling It All Together

Business Description

1. Describe your business.

2. State your company's mission

3. List your company's goals and future position within the industry.

4. Describe your company's business model and why it is unique to the industry.

   • Why are you going to be profitable?

   • Why will you succeed?

   • What direct experience does your management team have? If not direct, how relevant will their experience be to your business or industry? What do they offer to the business?

   • Have you talked with prospective or current customers? What are their comments?

   • Have you talked with competitors?

   • Is your business a quantity or quality business? At what volumes will you break even? Make a profit? Lose money?

   • Has your product or service matured within the industry?

   • How many industry turns do you expect every 6 months? Every 12 months?

   • What is the shelf life of your product?

   • When do you plan to open your doors for business?

   • Is your business seasonal in nature with peaks and valleys in selling cycles or will you have continuous selling year-round?

   • What are the days or hours you will be open? Will you be open nights, weekends or holidays? Why were these hours of operation chosen? Will you offer flexible or summer hours to employees?

   • How critical is your business location to customers or principal suppliers?

Outline Your Strategy

What is your company's strategy?

   • short-term goals

   • long-term goals

Product and Service Description

- Describe the uniqueness of your business in general terms.
- Describe the product, including physical characteristics, weight, size, color, packaging, etc.
- Provide a detailed description of the manufacturing process of the product. Give a timeline that identifies the various stages of research, development and production.
- Have you set up suppliers or distributors? Will they give you assistance?
- What credit terms are you going to make?
- Describe your services. If you offer more than one service, outline each service in detail.
- What does your service deliver?
- What is the primary application of your service? What is the secondary application?
- What need does it fill?
- Who are the customers?
- Who makes the buying decision? If the buyer and the user are different, what is the relationship between them?
- What are the customer benefits?
- What makes it different?
- Emphasize the product's/service's differences.
- State advantages and disadvantages of the product/service.
- State strengths/weaknesses of the product/service.
- How difficult or easy is the product to use from the user's standpoint?
- What are the results from using it?
- Why will the customer buy it?
- What types of regulations are relevant and affect the production, sales or use of the product?
- Is training needed to use it? To sell it? Describe the training needed and how you provide the training.
- Do you have any patents, trademarks, copyrights, etc.?
- What ancillary products are available with the product/service?
- What stage of development are you in with your product/service?
- What is the price sensitivity?
- How will the product be manufactured?
- What is your unique selling point?
- What is your product's/service's life cycle?

The Business History and Your Experience

1. Describe the status of your business—whether you are an existing business trying to attract investors to expand or you are starting a new company. State your targeted startup date or when you expect to secure funding.

2. Outline the legal structure of your company—where your company was founded, whether you are incorporated and the state in which you were incorporated. If you changed your incorporation status, show how and why your company status has changed.

3. Provide the names of all founding principals, stockholders and directors. If any changes have been made recently, mention all changes. If you have made any changes in the structure, management or ownership of the company, describe these changes in a brief and factual manner.

4. List any milestones and setbacks. Include a brief description of your lucky breaks or the mild setbacks you may have suffered while starting the business. Describe how these occurrences have helped to form your current ideas or offerings.

Trends and Technology

1. Describe how future trends will affect your business.
2. Cite any significant changes in technology that may affect your product or service.
3. Show how technology has enabled you to provide a product or service cheaper and faster or how increased competition is making it more difficult for you to compete.

Critical Risks and Opportunities

Define any potential risks and opportunities your company will face, both internally and externally.

Conduct a SWOT Analysis

- Identify your company's strengths.

- Identify your company's weaknesses.

- List all available opportunities.

- List each threat.

Intellectual Property

- Include copies of all patent, trademark, service mark and copyright applications submitted to the USPTO.

- Provide a status report for each application.

- Include a brief description of why an application was filed for each.

5 Analyzing Your Market

Overview

Before launching any type of promotion, you need to know who you are targeting, what your competition is offering and how you will market for maximum sales. What do you know about your customers, your competition and the markets you serve? Like most entrepreneurs, you think you know who your main competitors are and what they offer. But that is only one piece of the puzzle. How well do you know and understand your target market audience?

Thoroughly understanding your market, customers and competition is an important component of every business plan. Knowing in advance how many customers you can target, who they are, who your main competitors are and the state of the industry is also key information you will need to build a targeted marketing plan. A marketing plan is not complete if it lacks detailed descriptions of target markets followed by an analysis of the trends and conditions of the general marketplace and how these trends may affect the outcome and profitability of your business. The more information you arm yourself with, the better your chances of meeting your customers' needs and capturing the market.

This chapter will discuss the complete marketing process so that you will have all the information you need to create a winning marketing plan.

Analyzing Your Market, Competition, Customer and the Consumer

This section will take a look at different segments:

- market analysis
- competitive analysis
- customer analysis
- the consumer

Chapter 3 discussed how to find out what is going on in your industry and how to spot industry trends. This section will explore and analyze your market, competition and customers.

Market Analysis

Market analysis is a process of determining and defining the characteristics of the market you will be targeting for sales and the measurement of the market's capacity to buy your products and services. In other words, the analysis identifies and quantifies the customers you will be targeting for sales. A market analysis may also be referred to as an industry analysis or market overview.

Understanding both the strength and size of the market you will be competing for and your competition will help you better formulate and shape your plans. Whether you are a local business that services a local market or a national business, you need to know your current market, your competition, customer needs, emerging markets and marketing trends to be successful.

The Market

The market is a clearly defined group of people, area or group of things that can be classified together as having an element of commonality.

Define and describe the overall market you will be competing in. If applicable, break your overall markets into smaller groups for each geographical area you service: local, regional, national and international.

To help you define your target markets, you may need to do some research. There are a number of government and industry statistics available. Some sources include government Web sites, associations, directories and data compilation companies. You should frequently cite numbers and statistics and be prepared to explain how you reached each assumption. When drawing conclusions, support how the conclusion was reached. If you collect a large amount of facts and figures, it is easy to forget where a specific fact may have come from, so always keep copies of backup information. Be sure you can verify every finding. Verification may come from focus groups, articles in magazines, trade publications, newspapers, book references, research data or customer surveys.

Always source your information and always cross-check any statistic and review your market objectively. It is likely that you could discover a new market you did not even know existed, and this new information may set you on an entirely different course.

To help you define your overall market, answer each question carefully and objectively.

Define Your Overall Market

What is the total size of your intended market? (Break each region into a primary, secondary and tertiary market.)	Primary (your most obvious and most promising market)	Secondary (a new market with good potential)	Tertiary (an untried and untapped market)
Local			
Regional			
National			
International			
What are historical, current and projected growth rates?			
Historical			
Current			
Projected			
What social, economic or political changes may affect the market for your product or service?			
What changing needs do you see in the use of your product or service?			
Are there any independent industry or market studies available that you can source?			
Describe any recent product, service or industry developments.			
List any identifiable market niches for your product or service.			
What are or will be your customers' needs and desires?			
Are there natural borders you need to consider such as rivers, bridges or highways?			
Are there any common characteristics that customers in your target market share?			
How will customers learn about your product or service?			
What kind of advertising are they responsive to?			
What do existing customers like best about your product or service?			

Who else has a need for the product?			
Will you be offering the type of product or service they will buy?			
Are your target markets consumers or businesses or both?			

Hint

Conducting an overall market analysis even if you are servicing a small niche may bring to mind new business opportunities or market or product expansion ideas.

Identifying markets provides a snapshot of the target market that will be most interested in your product or service and provides you with the information you need to effectively market your product or service.

The next step after determining your markets is to identify new industry or market trends by reviewing news clippings, government reports, consumer spending reports and analysts' predictions.

Industry Trends

Almost every business within a segment is influenced by industry trends. These are major trends such as an increase in service businesses and a decrease of manufacturing in the United States. It may also include major influences such as the high reliance on the Internet by consumers, to name a few.

Target Market Trends

Trends can be influenced by demographics such as age, income or changing migration patterns by individuals more than 50 years old or less than 30 years old. It can also include cultural and social influences such as the increased number of assisted living facilities or the increased number of individuals who purchase products online.

Sometimes a market or industry change may appear to happen overnight. Market changes may take years and can often come quietly and over time. Pay attention to small but subtle changes in your industry or changing market trends. You can spot changes by conducting your own database analysis or sending a survey to customers or prospects. Surveys may be conducted online or via telephone to obtain an immediate snapshot of forming trends.

Hint

Pay close attention to changes in industry or market trends. A careful analysis of changes in the market should be reviewed as you create your plan. Even small demographic changes such as the building of a new residential housing development or new retail mall nearby can have a big impact on your projected revenues. Also be on the lookout for emerging new markets, competitive changes and shifting demographics. Although changes may be subtle and seem unimportant, small changes may cause you to overlook an important market segment.

Competitive Analysis

Competitive analysis is the comparison of businesses that compete for your customers at a local or national level. In this exercise, you will identify competitors and analyze everything associated with their products and services, such as product quality, pricing, customer service, marketing strengths or weaknesses, etc.

Competition Identification

Every product has competition. Competition can be divided into two types: direct and indirect. Who are your direct competitors? Competition can also be defined as: primary—companies that offer the same products and services as you and to the same markets; and secondary—companies that offer products and services that have some similarities to yours but do not compete for the same market; or tertiary—companies that offer complementary products or services that are related to your product or service offering and may be channeling sales away from your company.

To build a competitive analysis you need to understand who your competition is. Make a list of all competitors and break them into two columns:

My Competition

Direct	Indirect

Next, determine the size of the companies that compete with you. Size may be determined by number of employees, unit sales or sales volume.

My Competition

Size	Direct	Indirect

Use this listing of competitors to build a competitive analysis.

Direct and Indirect Competition

Direct Competition

A direct or primary competitor offers products that provide the same benefits and results as yours. Direct competitors offer similar products or services to exactly the same market or audience that you are targeting.

Indirect Competition

Indirect or secondary competitors are companies that offer products or services that the customer or consumer could buy instead of yours. The products or services are not exactly the same as yours, but offer the same benefits and results.

Know Your Competition

The better you know your competition the better you can differentiate your company from your competitors. Develop a comprehensive competitive analysis worksheet to study your competition. Break your competition into the three groups (primary, secondary and tertiary). Gather information on your direct competitors first, then research information about your indirect competitors. The key to creating a balanced and objective analysis is to stick to the facts and be sure that you can back up any substantive facts.

There are a number of sources of information you can tap into to learn more about your competition:

- Visit your competitor's site. Note the physical appearance of the building, the customers who enter, the location of the building, etc. Through general observation you can learn a lot about your competition and its customers.

- Become a customer of your competition. Buying your competitor's products brings you directly into your competitor's database. You will receive first-hand information about the quality of their products, any new products scheduled to be launched, how they promote, how they charge for their product or service and if they give preferred treatment to customers.

- Conduct an Internet search. A wealth of information is available today through the Internet. Start by looking up the company name or product using popular search engines. Most established companies are public corporations that must publicly file corporate earnings and losses with the U.S. Securities and Exchange Commission.

- Online media and newsgroups provide additional sources of online information:
  –Inc. 500 (www.inc.com)
  –NewsDirectory.com (www.newsdirectory.com)

As you collect competitive information, you may be surprised at how much you will learn about your competition. You may be surprised to learn that a company you thought was an indirect competitor is now a direct competitor. For each competitor, complete a detailed profile including the following information.

Competitive Analysis Worksheet

A sample competitive analysis worksheet is located in the Planning Worksheets section and on the Web landing page www.socrates.com/books/business-plan.aspx.

Is the company status private or public?	
What is the size of the company that may compete with you?	
What other products do they sell?	
Who are they selling to?	

Review comparisons on trends in their sales, market share and profitability.	
What is their pricing? Are you higher? Are you lower?	
Compare warranties, performance, service, distribution and product features.	
Compare managerial, financial, marketing and operational strengths and weaknesses.	
How does your product/service stack up to the competition's?	
What are the key features and benefits of its product/service?	
What is its pricing structure? How much does it charge for their product/service?	
Is the competition adequately financed and on sound financial footing?	
What is its approach to marketing? How often or how much does it promote its product/service?	
How does it promote its product/service?	
Has it announced new product initiatives?	
What is the potential for future competitors to enter the market and create more competition?	
What are their weaknesses?	
Do they compete on price, service or technology?	

Summarize the information in a spreadsheet or table using a consistent format. Competitors may be listed in alphabetical order or by level of competition to your business. To keep up with your competition, review and update the information every 4–6 months. Markets are constantly changing and so is your competition. If you are not paying attention, competition may pop up right next door.

Look for trends or holes in your or a competitor's product line, including pricing discrepancies, marketing changes, new product development, etc. Study what your competitors offer versus what you offer. If you offer a similar product, how do your products differ? What do they offer that you do not and vice versa?

Take your time to conduct thorough research. A good analysis can take up to 40 hours or more to research and document. Again, it is important to remain objective. Realizing that your competition has comparable or possibly better product, warranty or customer service policies than you is useful information.

Utilize this information in a positive way to improve your own product. What does the competitor offer that you do not? Dismissing potential competition may be very harmful to your future business plans. If your field is already crowded with competition, your research will tell you whether the market can sustain your business or if the field is too crowded and will make it difficult for you to succeed.

There are a number of reliable sources already available to you to help you locate information about your competitors. Information can be gathered from:

- searching association listings
- viewing directory listings
- attending trade shows
- talking with sales reps
- reviewing promotional materials
- surveying your current customers
- visiting competitors' Web sites
- Edgar Online—SEC filing information (www.edgaronline.gov)
- market research company databases (for example: www.hooversonline.com, Dunn & Bradstreet, Experian, to name a few)
- reading trade publications
- signing up for your competitors' mailing lists or online newsletters
- requesting brochures or catalogs from your competitors (if applicable)

Market Share

Sales figures are a good indicator of how well a company is performing, especially if sales dramatically fluctuate from year to year; but they do not necessarily indicate how a company is performing relative to its competitors. In reality, sales fluctuations may reflect changes in the market size or changes in economic conditions.

A company's performance relative to its competitors can only be measured by the proportion of the market that the company is able to capture. This proportion is referred to as the company's market share.

Market share may be determined through one of two ways:

Overall Market Share

A company's overall market share is its sales expressed as a percentage of total market sales. Two decisions are necessary to use this measure. The first is whether to use unit sales or dollar sales. The second is defining the total market. (For example: A national bicycle company's share of the bicycle market depends on whether trick bikes, motorized bikes or off-road bikes are included in the total market. If all of the above types of bikes are included in the calculation, then the bicycle company's share will be smaller than if the calculation was based on just one segment of the total bicycle market.)

Served Market Share

A company's served market share is its sales expressed as a percentage of the total sales to its served market. Its served market consists of all the buyers who would be able and willing to buy its product. (For example: If a major bicycle company only produced and sold expensive bicycles on the East Coast, its served market share would be its sales percentage of the total sales of expensive bicycles sold on the East Coast. A company could capture 100 percent of its served market and yet have a relatively small share of the total market.)

Calculate Your Market Share

The formula to calculate your market share is simple: Take the total sales of your business and divide that number by the total sales of your industry for either your local market or national or international market. The resulting number shows how much of the total market you have captured.

Sales may be determined on a value basis (sales price multiplied by volume) or on a unit basis (number of units shipped or number of customers served).

Use this calculation to determine how much market share you have captured. If you have captured more than half of the markets you serve, consider expanding your markets or creating new products or services to promote into a new market. If you have captured only a small portion of your overall market, review your marketing mix to help you capture a larger portion of the market.

> **Market Share = Company's Sales / Total Market Sales**
>
> **Or**
>
> **Market Share = Company's Sales / Total Sales to Its Served Market**

Knowing how much of the market you have or will capture will influence your future marketing efforts.

- What percent of total sales in your market area do you expect to obtain after your business is in full operation?

- What percent of the total market share must be taken away from your competition in order to reach your projected market share?

- What sales volume do you expect to reach with your products or services in 1 year, 2 years and 3 years?

Market Share Calculation

The number of consumers who purchased toothpaste last year (1,000,000)	x	Annual consumer consumption by unit (6 tubes of toothpaste each per year)	=	Total market size (6,000,000 tubes produced each year)
Total market size (6,000,000 tubes purchased last year)	/	Your average annual unit sales (you sell 200,000 tubes each year)	=	Your market share (3.3%)

Why is market share important? Typically, a higher market share generates a higher return on investment (ROI).

Market Share to ROI Correlations

Market share (percent)	ROI (percent)
Less than 7	10
7+–15	16
15+–23	21
23+–38	23
38+	33

The reverse is true as well—a loss in market share leads to a decline in ROI.

Reasons to Increase Your Market Share

Economies of scale–Higher volume can be key in developing a cost advantage.

Sales growth in a stagnant industry–When the industry is not growing, your company can still grow sales by increasing your market share.

Reputation–Market leaders have clout that they can use to their advantage.

Increased bargaining power–A larger player has an advantage in negotiations with suppliers and channel members.

Your company may gain market share by offering a product or service that differentiates you from your competitors. The offering may be lower pricing, better quality, better service, longer warranties, etc. Which of the following factors give your company an edge over your competition?

- You use innovative technology.
- You offer superior customer service.
- You have low marketing costs.
- You have high profit potential.
- Customers perceive your product to be of higher quality.
- A small number of competing companies provide the same product or service, yet the overall market size is large enough to sustain multiple companies.
- You have the ability to capture 20 to 40 percent of the market.
- There are no seasonal fluctuations that may be deemed as an obstacle.

Reasons Not to Increase Your Market Share

An increase of market share is not always desirable. For example:

- If your company is at production capacity, an increase in market share might necessitate a capital investment in additional capacity. If demand decreases and the new capacity is underutilized, higher costs will result.
- Overall profits may decline if market share is gained by increasing promotional expenditures or by decreasing prices.
- A price war may be started if competitors attempt to regain their share by lowering prices.
- A small niche player may be tolerated if it captures only a small share of the market. If that share increases, a larger, more capable competitor may decide to enter the niche.
- Antitrust issues may arise if a firm dominates its market.

In some cases, it may be advantageous to decrease market share. For example, if your company identifies certain customers as unprofitable, you may choose to drop those customers and lose market share to improve profitability.

Learning the Language of Business

Readers are entitled to full access and use of the comprehensive Business Law and Accounting & Finance Dictionaries found on the Web landing page at www.socrates.com/books/business-plan.aspx. Please remember to register the first time you use this free resource. See page iv for instructions.

Increasing Your Market Share

The market share of a product can be modeled as:

Share of Market = Share of Preference x Share of Voice x Share of Distribution

According to this model, there are three components of market share:

- Share of Preference—can be increased through product, pricing and promotional changes.

- Share of Voice—the company's proportion of total promotional expenditures in the market. Thus, share of voice can be increased by increasing advertising expenditures.

- Share of Distribution—can be increased through more intensive distribution (more distributors, hiring more salespeople, greater promotion, etc.).

Customer Analysis

Customer analysis is the process of analyzing your current customer demographics, psychographics and purchasing habits. You will learn who your current customers are; what they purchase; where and how they purchase; how much they spend on each sale; how often they purchase from you; where they live; their gender and age; the number of active customer accounts, etc. Armed with this information you can develop new products, locate new market niches and cross-promote products to existing customers. But what if you are just starting out and have not acquired customers yet? A customer analysis is still a necessary step and valuable tool for every new business. Instead of analyzing existing customers, you will be, in effect, analyzing who you think your ideal customer should be.

Who is or will be your customer? Develop a customer profile to determine who your target market is.

Preparing a Customer Profile to Define Your Market

Define the customer who will buy your product or services.

1. Who are your customers? What is their economic makeup? Include demographic statistics, charts and tables if available. What is their age, nationality, sex, religion or political views?

2. What is their education level, occupation, marital status and size of family?

3. Where do they live or work?

4. Do they work for a Fortune 100, 500 or 1000 corporation? Are they sole proprietors, small businesses, individual contractors or consumers?

5. What is the size of your potential market?

6. Do they purchase more than one item or service at a time?

7. What influences their purchasing decisions—price, quality, size, availability, warranties, service, discounts, color, payment terms?

8. Where do they make their purchases—by catalog, Internet, phone, in person?

9. Is the product or service necessary, optional or a luxury?

10. How is the product or service used by the customer?

11. Is their purchase seasonal or year round?

12. Does one person make the buying decision or is a committee involved?

13. How long is the decision making process?

14. Are the buyer and user the same person?

Collect as much information about your customers as you can to develop a comprehensive picture of the types of customers you will be marketing to. One of the best methods of obtaining this information is to survey your current and potential customers. Conduct a customer survey to determine who you are marketing to. Where are your customers found? Why do they purchase your product over your competitor's? What is their economic makeup?

Customer Survey

Query past, current and potential customers, incorporating various responses from the different mediums you sell through or plan to sell through. Ask frontline workers, customer service, etc. to ask customers when they have them on the phone, through live Internet chat, etc.

Distributing the Survey

- Mail a survey to households within a geographic area. Include a postage-paid response card that the recipient fills out then sends back.

- Telephone customers.

- Ask customers when talking to them on the phone.

- Include a survey with monthly statements or invoices.

- Hang door hangers on resident's front doors.

- Post a survey on your company's Web site.

Customer Survey Questions

What are the main reasons you purchase our product or service?
How do you view our competition?
What are the main benefits you receive or expect to receive?
What do you think sets us apart from our competitors?
How satisfied are you with our customer service?
Are our reps friendly?
Do you always find what you need?
How is our return policy?
Who do you consider to be our competition?
What do you prefer about their product or service?
What do you like better about ours?
How do our prices compare?
How does our service compare?
Why do you shop here?

Understanding the Customer

To understand customer needs, ask these types of questions:

What could we do to make your buying experience more valuable?
How have our products or services helped you?
Why did you stop buying from us?
What are your immediate needs?
What are the issues you will be facing within the next 12 months?

Customer Needs

Does your product or service solve a need for your customer? Determining your customers' needs will help you provide the product or service they want. Conducting a customer needs analysis will define the needs of your customers and will direct the type of product or service you should provide.

When conducting your needs analysis, be highly specific about the benefits the customer will derive from the purchase of the product or service. What needs does it fulfill? Include all benefits: direct, indirect, tangible and intangible.

- What are your customers' needs?

- What primary need does this product fulfill?

- What other needs does it fulfill?

- How many other companies fulfill this need for the customer?

- How is my product/service different than the competition?

What if you discover a considerable hole in fulfilling a customer need? Look carefully, most customer needs do not go unattended for very long. If there is currently a hole, it may mean the need really is not great enough to be profitable, the need is not as large as it may have initially seemed or your competition is already making plans to move into the marketplace.

Market Segments

Market segments are the logical breakdown and grouping of customers or customer needs or products. They may also be called market niches.

Identifying Niches

Identifying niches is similar to carving out a small slice of an otherwise big piece of pie. It involves identifying and creating a place in the market where no one else is, thus providing a need that no one else is serving. Selling to a niche market allows you to sell your product within a segment of the market that is often free from competition. A niche market allows you to define who you are marketing to. It is usually used by smaller firms as they can concentrate on establishing a strong image and position in their niche. This lets you own a piece of the market that no one else owns, where you can establish your own brand before competition recognizes your niche and moves in.

Often small business owners view a niche market as narrowing their sales or cutting into a profit margin, so they fear it. The truth is a niche market could be defined as a component that gives your business greater power.

Developing New Niches

Niche marketing can be extremely cost-effective. Imagine offering a product or service that is just right for a select demographic group such as sports fans or businesses in your area. You could advertise on targeted sports or all news format radio stations, which have considerably lower rates than stations that program for broader audiences. Thus, your marketing budget would go a lot further, allowing you to advertise with greater frequency or to use a more comprehensive media mix.

Testing new niche markets can be a low-risk way to grow your business, as long as you keep in mind several important rules:

Meet a Unique Need

The benefits from the product or service you promised must have specific appeal to the market niche. What can you provide that is new, different and compelling? In order for niche marketing to be effective, you must identify the unique needs of your potential audience and look for ways to tailor your product or service to meet them.

To determine if a product or service will meet a unique need, start by considering all the product or service variations you might offer. Make sure you are meeting the three most important criteria: Is the product or service unique? Is it compelling? Is it fulfilling a void in the market?

Speak the Language

When approaching a new market niche, it is imperative to speak its language. In other words, understand the market's hot buttons and be prepared to communicate with the target group as an understanding member—not an outsider. In addition to launching a unique campaign for the new niche, keep in mind you may need to alter other, more basic elements, such as your company slogan if it translates poorly into another language, for example.

Make the Message Specific

To succeed in a niche market it is important to understand key communication issues. To successfully increase sales from the new niche, the marketer may need to change the way it communicates with the niche market by revising its broad marketing message to communicate specific benefits and features to the niche group.

Research before You Launch

Before entering the new market, assess the direct competitors and determine how you will position yourself against them. For an overview of the market, conduct a competitive analysis by reviewing competitors' ads, brochures and Web sites, looking for their key selling points, along with pricing, delivery and other service characteristics.

But what if you cannot find existing competition? Believe it or not, this is not always a good sign. While it may mean that other companies have not identified your specific niche yet, it is also possible that many companies have tried and failed to penetrate this group. Always test market carefully to gauge the market's receptiveness to your product or service and message. And move cautiously to keep your risks manageable.

Locating Niche Markets

To determine if there are other niche markets you are overlooking, review your customer list carefully for hidden trends. Is there a customer type that has not been promoted to in the past that can be tapped? An example is the over 50 market or 16- to 18-year-olds. Maybe you now carry products that appeal to these age groups.

For business markets, are there vertical markets you are missing? Architecture, publishing, legal, etc. Maybe a good look at the titles of the people purchasing your products will reveal a missed marketing opportunity.

One effective, inexpensive method of reaching new markets is to look for synergies in your own services by looking for others with whom you can partner to cross-promote products, conduct a seminar or publish a newsletter.

Vertical Niche Markets

- Are there vertical markets you might be overlooking?

- Look for synergies in your own services by looking for others with whom you can partner to cross-promote products, conduct a seminar or publish a white paper.

Talk to your customers. Your potential customers may tell you what is missing in your competitors' products and services. They may also tell you what you need to do to gain their business.

Consumer Analysis

Consider this: The customer may not always be the consumer and vice versa. Most entrepreneurs overlook the important fact that the person purchasing the product may not, in fact, be the end user. Look carefully at your markets. Who is actually doing the buying? Is it a parent, a grandparent, a boss or business owner? Who is the actual end user? Is it a son or daughter, or an employee? Analyze how the product is being used. Is it being used by the purchaser, or is it being purchased as a gift? Understanding who the customer is and who the consumer is presents an important distinction and will make a big difference in determining how the product or service is marketed and sold.

Pulling It All Together

Build a Competitive Analysis Worksheet

1. List your primary, secondary and tertiary competitors.

2. What products or services do they offer?

3. What do they charge?

4. How do competing companies sell their product or service?

5. List competitor's strengths.

6. List competitor's weaknesses.

Summarize Your Market

1. List any industry trends you identified.

2. List any market trends you identified.

3. List your direct competition.

4. List your indirect competition.

5. What is your market share?

6. What is your overall market share?

7. What is your served market share?

8. Who is your customer?

9. How often do customers purchase from you?

10. What is the average unit of sale of each purchase?

11. What does your primary customer profile look like?

12. What are their traits?

- geographics
- demographics
- psychographics

13. List your customers' needs.

14. Describe how you fill these needs for your customers.

15. List three new niche markets you have identified.

6 Your Marketing Strategy

The Marketing Strategy

Only after you have analyzed and determined your customer needs, competition and markets, can you begin building a comprehensive marketing strategy. Your marketing strategy is the overall approach and direction your business will take to meet your business goals and objectives.

Your marketing strategy will integrate all activities involved in marketing—sales, advertising, multimedia and online, networking and public relations. Each of these components will complement each other to enhance your company image and to set you apart from your competition.

> "Some entrepreneurs think they have the product that everyone will beat down the door to get. You may have the greatest product available, but if you do not have a good way to market it or get the word out, nobody will know about it, and you will not have the sales."
>
> **Curtis Roeschley**
> **Director**
> **Jane Addams Hull House Association**
> **Small Business Development Center**
> **Chicago, IL**

Marketing Strategy Goals

What do you hope to accomplish with your marketing strategy? Would you like to increase your customer database by 25 percent? Increase the average unit sale by 20 percent? Increase profitability by 10 percent? Each goal should be specific and measurable, and each goal should be explained in specific terms. If your goals are not achieved within a planned schedule, review your marketing plan to determine which components should be reassessed or redesigned to meet your goals. Incorporate your marketing strategy goals into your marketing plan.

Your Marketing Plan

Why develop a marketing plan? Everyone needs a marketing plan. A marketing plan is a long-term roadmap of strategic and tactical objects that result in a positioning of your company and products in support of your 62.

> **A marketing plan is composed from three objectives:**
>
> 1. **Strategic objectives**–Objectives that set the foundation for the execution of tactical objectives. With strategic objectives, you attempt to manipulate or create the environment in which the product or service will be sold.
>
> 2. **Tactical objectives**–Tangible, measurable tasks that must be accomplished to further the strategic objectives. Example: You plan to exhibit at a national trade show with the intent of acquiring 50 new qualified sales leads, one press interview, meetings with 10 current customers and 15 potential customers, and industry press coverage.
>
> 3. **Overall objective**–Your company's overall objective is to create stakeholder value. The focus may be on creating name or brand recognition, new customer acquisition, customer retention or attracting investors. The objective of your marketing plan may change over time.

Developing a Marketing Plan

Detailing your marketing plan ensures that the different aspects of your marketing are not carried out in isolation. A marketing plan is a roadmap to developing a successful marketing campaign. The most successful marketing strategies complement and reinforce one another.

A well-designed marketing plan will provide a timeline of objectives and events that help your company reach your overall objective. A marketing plan is strategic in nature. It requires the support, consent and commitment of management at all levels and must be viewed as furthering the interest of the customer. Consider the marketing mix carefully, or the plan will result in a disappointing outcome. Include these components in your marketing plan to develop a well-balanced plan:

Three Years' Sales Projections or Results (Net Sales, Percentage Change)

Include a brief calendar of the past year, highlighting the main events including successes and failures. Use the overview to look at how past trends might continue into the future. Include the past year's sales results by marketing channel, if available.

Goals and Objectives

Give an objective, or several objectives. These could be in terms of revenue, number of sales or customers, or you could set quantifiable marketing goals—such as opening a new shop. Objectives may also include product concept—such as product definition. What is it? What is the purpose of the product? How is it used? How often is it to be delivered? What is the price? Include your preliminary market identification.

Give the benefit of the product/service to customers. What problem does it solve for the customer? Describe the need for this product from the customer's perspective. Define its impact on the customer. How will your customers sell or justify this product to management or use the product themselves?

Can customers currently obtain this product or service more cost-effectively than you can provide it? What would compel customers to change from the product/service they are currently using to the product described in your plan?

What do you want your marketing program to accomplish—acquiring new customers; increasing current customer purchases; reactivating lapsed customers; launching a new product; or tying your marketing goals and budgets to your business goals?

Strategies and Tactics

Develop your strategies, then create a list of tactics to get there.

Strategies—What you want to achieve. A strategy may include increasing market share by 10 percent and increasing the Return On Investment (ROI) by 16 percent. Another strategy may be to increase the average customer purchase by five percent (without raising prices.)

Tactics—What you need to create to achieve the strategy.

Product/Service

Define the impact of this new product/service on other products you offer—positive or negative—and describe how this product fits in with other products/services in the product line. What currently offered products/services can be used with this product?

Identify and describe the risks associated with this product/service. How is the product/service sold? What kind of sales support is provided? What additional staff and/or training is required to support the product/service? Through what other channels could this product/service be sold? What would be required for this to happen?

Detail promotions planned for the year by month, quantity, costs and expected response and sales.

New Product Launch

Detail new product launches planned for the year. Include key dates, costs, sales goals, etc.

Market Research

> **Detail market definitions.** How does the product/service relate to the mission and strategic direction of your company? Who would use this product/service? Who are the customers for this product by industry/category? Estimate the number of customers by category or industry—by size and rank. What is the current level of customer acceptance or understanding of this type of product?
>
> **Include competitive information.** Is there a competitive product/service on the market? If so, how do your products/services differ? What does your competition charge for its product? Describe your competitor's selling strategy. Does this product/service compete with any of your existing products/services? If so, how? Are there any competing products/services sold by other companies on the same topic but in different forms? How does the product/service relate to the mission and strategic direction of your company?

Pricing

Summarize your latest pricing calculations. Include special offer pricing, introductory pricing, multiple discount or wholesale pricing. Record the pricing of your competitors at the same time.

Sales Plan

Include a comprehensive statement on how the sales are to be achieved to meet the targets mentioned previously in Goals and Objectives. Describe the readiness of the project, the timing of its launch and what launch publicity you are planning. Include as much detail as possible and a timetable. Review your distribution, sales responsibilities, monitoring and sales strategies.

Advertising, Promotion and PR

Specify in detail what advertising, promotion and PR you are planning for the year ahead. Spread promotions by month.

Budget/Financials

Include a calculation of how much the marketing budget should be for the year ahead.

Cash Flow Forecast

Spread expected sales and costs by month for the year ahead. The budget will relate directly to likely advertising, and other promotions. Include an estimated profit and loss (P&L) calculation for each promotion planned.

Marketing Communications (PR and the Marketing Mix)

Developing Your Marketing Mix

- Include networking in your overall marketing mix. Word of mouth is a powerful tool.
- Include PR in your overall marketing mix. It is a great way to gain national exposure at minimal costs. The secret to getting your item printed in magazines and newspapers is the "hook"—what you are promoting, why it is important, what it will do for the consumer, how it ties into the audience and how it is different from other like products.
- Balance your marketing channels—advertising space, e-mail, PR, direct mail, direct response, telephone, promotional pieces/giveaways, Web, Yellow Pages, etc. Remember to give your marketing materials a chance to work.
- Your marketing efforts do not have to be grandiose, they just need to be sustainable. Do a little something every month. Efficient, inexpensive monthly programs include:
    - inserts into the local paper
    - product stuffers into product shipments
    - e-mail
    - postcards to customers
    - Point-of-Purchase (POP) signs on counters, etc.
    - billboards
    - printed shopping bags
    - bus and taxi advertisement
    - space ads
    - street banners
    - new resident welcome gifts
    - trade shows/fairs/consumer shows
    - door-to-door saturation—door hangers and handouts
    - Internet
    - coupon mailers
    - networking
    - press releases
    - giveaways that are viewable daily—magnets, rulers, paperweights, bags
    - customer surveys
    - sponsorship
    - Customer Relationship Management or Customer Retention Marketing (CRM) programs

Pricing Strategies

Pricing is often viewed as the measurement of a product's or service's worth. The more expensive the item, the greater the perceived value, even if it is of comparable quality to a less expensive model or service. In the end, the customer is willing to pay a price that is consistent with his or her perceived value of the offering.

There are different pricing strategies you can implement when introducing a new product:

- Cost-Based Pricing is calculated by determining the costs of producing a product or service then adding a profit margin.
- Cost Plus Profit is calculated by taking the cost of the product or service and adding a desired profit percentage that is reasonable to your industry onto the price.
- Market-Based Pricing is determined by studying your competition's pricing and how customers decide what and when to buy to fix the price of your offering. Market-based pricing is more complicated to calculate, but it produces the most profit on each sale.

Answer these key questions when determining your pricing strategies:

1. How much flexibility do you have in your pricing strategy?

2. What is the lowest price you can charge to cover the cost of your product or service?

   - What is the highest price your target market will bear?

   - How should you price your product/service?

   - Should it be higher or lower than your competitors?

Hint

Price is important but is not the main reason people make purchases. Price and perceived value go hand in hand.

New Product Introduction Pricing

When introducing new products or services there are three pricing strategies to choose from:

Premium Pricing

This is when you set the price higher than your competition in an attempt to appeal to the customers who are more motivated to pay a higher price. There is a segment of the market that will associate a higher priced product or service with better quality—although that assumption is not always accurate. Premium pricing may drive away price sensitive buyers and produce fewer unit sales, but it will also increase your profit margin. This strategy works well when there is little or no competition to your product or service, or you are offering a unique, one-of-a-kind or hard to obtain product or service.

Market Penetration Pricing

Offering an introductory rate is most common when introducing a new product or service, and the intent is to quickly grab market share from the more established competition. This type of pricing involves lowering your price to a level below your competition's to gain immediate name recognition and to attract your competitor's buyers. Once buyers have been acquired and have become comfortable or attached to the new product or service, a company may increase the price to be equal to the competition. Price sensitive purchasers will be attracted to this pricing strategy, whereas the quality conscious buyer will view the quality with suspicion and will be reluctant to switch.

Parallel Pricing

This strategy is created to offer the product or service at the exact same price as your competition. The pricing decision is made to interest buyers of your competitor's product or service to take a look at you. This encourages buyers to compare your product or service feature by feature to your competitor's. This strategy works well if your product can withstand the comparison test.

Mature Product/Service Pricing

Product and service pricing is fluid and should be reviewed periodically. As marketing conditions change, so should your pricing strategies. It is not recommended that you change your pricing structure too frequently, but it is advisable to review your competitors' pricing for comparison. Pricing is a marketing strategy, and as markets change, so should your pricing strategies.

Set Your Price

Use the following worksheet to determine the best price for your service or product for maximum profits. This worksheet is also included in Chapter 20: Planning Worksheets.

Setting Prices for Maximum Profits

Describe how you determined your present/proposed pricing structure:
_____
_____

How does your pricing compare to the competition? _____
_____
_____

If you are higher, list the advantages your products/services have over the competition:_____
_____

If you are lower, list the advantages of the competitor's products/services over your product: _____

_____

_____

For each product, review your profit calculations. Have you covered all expenses related to the development or offering of the product or service? Consider all costs on a per unit basis:

- Materials (costs): _____

- Labor (cost per unit): _____

- Overhead expenses (a percentage of sales): _____

- Shipping costs (cost per unit): _____

- Handling costs (cost per unit): _____

- Storage (cost per unit): _____

For each service you provide, review your profit calculations. Have you covered all expenses related to the service offering?

- Hourly billing rates: _____

- Project by project estimates: _____

- Monthly retainer structure: _____

- Travel cost: _____

- Client support costs: _____

- Proposal development costs: _____

What is your lowest price? _____

What is your highest price? _____

Where does your current pricing fall? _____

Sales Strategies

Determine your online and offline sales strategy to reach your target market. Your marketing plan should identify how you plan to contact prospects, what materials you need to send or deliver and how follow-up will occur.

Promotion costs will vary widely depending on the type of effort you select and the frequency with which you promote. To determine how much you will need to appropriate for promotions, determine the cost of each sales/promotion medium to build your budget.

Bundling Products

If you are marketing more than one product or service, consider bundling them together at a bundled price. Example: If your main business is selling bicycles, but you also sell bicycle accessories–such as helmets, locks, gel seats, carrier compartments–consider bundling a number of products with the sale of each bicycle to create a complete bicycle kit. Because you are selling more than one product in the sale, you can bundle the products together for one low kit price and save the customer 15 to 20 percent over the cost of buying the products separately.

Budgeting for Marketing Activity

The Marketing Calendar

Determine monthly how you want to market, then develop a marketing plan that fits your budget. How much do you need to create a sustainable program? Marketing is a series of actions that continue indefinitely. Use the guidelines below or simply put aside a straight 10 percent of your gross monthly sales toward marketing.

Start with a typical annual marketing budgetary figure of five percent. For each factor in turn, work across the table, adding or subtracting percentage points depending on your own situation. If the factor is not relevant to your type of business, disregard it and move on to the next factor.

Table for Estimating a Marketing Budget

Factor	Add 2% for each appropriate factor	5% (typical figure)	Subtract 1% for each appropriate factor
Age of business	New	Young	Established
Age of product	New	Young	Established
Innovation level	Very innovative, customer needs educating	Some innovative details	None
Premises/ Location	Remote: level profile	Not remote or prime	Prime: high profile
Customers	Consumer	Consumer and business	Business
Agent/ Distributor network	None	Limited	Good coverage
Competition	Hostile	Benign	None
Special factors	Yes, more need to promote	None	Yes, less need to promote

The starting point of five percent is based on a percentage of forecasted sales. This shows that a budget of five percent on forecasted sales of $100,000 translates into a $5,000 marketing budget to cover advertising, promotion and PR but excludes the direct costs of salespeople. The five percent figure will fluctuate based on type of business, where you are located and type of customer. It can be increased as deemed necessary.

Examples of Estimating a Marketing Budget

Promotion Budget for a Retail Shop

A recently opened shop selling bicycles is located in a town center site–but not a prime location–and has limited competition. To work out their marketing budget, starting with five percent of their forecast turnover, the owners calculated as follows:

- age of business: new—add 2 percent
- age of product: not relevant
- innovation level: not relevant
- premises location: not remote or prime
- customers: consumers—add 2 percent
- agent/distributor network: not relevant
- competition: benign
- special factors: none

The owners, therefore, planned for a marketing budget of approximately: 5% + 2% + 2% = 9% of their forecasted sales for the product (or $9,000). When determining their startup costs, they should set aside $9,000 for carefully planned and highly targeted marketing promotions during the first 12 months or until sales reach monthly projections.

Promotion Budget for a Services Company

A small design firm that is 2 years old and in an out-of-the-way location is about to launch a new service for the paint industry. The company has a number of distributors, and there is no direct competitor. To get an idea as to how much the owners should budget for marketing the new device, the calculation would be as follows:

- age of business: young
- age of product: new—add 2 percent
- innovation level: very—add 2 percent
- premises location: not relevant
- customers: business—subtract 1 percent
- agent/distributor network: good coverage—subtract 1 percent
- competition: none—subtract 1 percent
- special factors: competition anticipated—add 2 percent

The firm's marketing budget should be: 5% + 2% + 2% - 1% - 1% - 1% + 2% = 8% of its likely sales of the new device.

For every dollar collected, the owners should put aside 8 cents toward future marketing programs.

The long form profit and loss statement tracks each cost for each promotion, providing you with a detailed snapshot of the effectiveness of your marketing strategy. Cost $/M refers to the cost per each thousand pieces.

Cost to Acquire a Customer and Profit Margin

To determine acquisition costs per customer, apply these simple calculations:

Assume you are spending 60 cents per mailing piece—total in-the-mail cost, printing, postage, letter shop, list rental—and getting 1.10 percent average response from rental files.

- cost to reach a prospect: $0.60

- average response: 1.10 percent

- cost to reach a prospect divided by average response = cost to acquire a customer

The cost to acquire a customer is:
$ 0.60 ÷ 1.10 percent = $54.55.

> "When you are doing the sales projections, your best source of information is your competition or a trade association in your industry or a shop owner next to where you want to be located or someone that has your same exact business but they are going after business in another part of the country."
>
> **Kelly Mizeur**
> **Finance Counselor**
> **Women's Business**
> **Development Center**
> **Chicago, IL**

Next, determine how much profit margin is earned on the average initial sales. By subtracting this amount from the cost to acquire a customer, you will know how much was initially invested in a new customer. Assume the average initial order of $70 and an average margin of 40 percent after fulfillment costs.

> "It is very difficult to project or put together good revenue assumptions. Expenses are easy. Do I need a location? How big does it have to be and [how] much will it cost me? Do I have to pay utilities? That is a line item—I need to hire an accountant. How much will that cost me? You can do that research; it is very easy and easier to figure out sales doing so."
>
> **Kelly Mizeur**
> **Finance Counselor**
> **Women's Business Development Center**
> **Chicago, IL**

- average initial order: $70

- average margin: 40 percent

- advertising cost to acquire a customer: $54.55

- average initial order x average margin = profit margin on initial sale

Profit margin earned on the average initial sale is: $70 x 40 percent = $28.00.

- advertising cost to acquire a customer–profit margin on initial sales = initial investment (per customer)

The initial cost to acquire a customer is: $54.55–$28.00 = $26.55.

Hint

Carefully incorporate telemarketing, e-mail marketing and faxes into your promotion mix. The federal government has instituted the National Do Not Call Registry. To learn more about the registry you can visit www.ftc.gov/donotcall. Many states have strict anti-spam laws in effect as well. Violators can be heavily fined unless a previous relationship has been established. To learn more, visit www.firstgov.gov to search for individual state laws.

Pulling It All Together

Now that you have completed all your research, it is time to pull it all together. Use this worksheet to develop your marketing strategy and plan.

Build a 12-month marketing plan integrating all promotion channels—marketing, sales, advertising, multimedia and online, networking and public relations.

List three strategic objectives of your marketing:

1. _____

2. _____

3. _____

For each strategic objective listed, describe the tactical objectives or tasks that must be accomplished to achieve each objective:

1. _____

2. _____

3. _____

Describe your overall marketing objectives:

1. _____

2. _____

3. _____

Project sales for the next 3 years:

Projected Sales Year 1: $ _____

Projected Sales Year 2: $ _____

Projected Sales Year 3: $ _____

What do you want your marketing program to accomplish? Tie your marketing goals and budgets to your business goals.

- Acquiring new customers?

- Increasing current customer purchases?

- Launching a new product?

Detail new product launches planned for the year. Provide a timeline for introducing new products during the next 12 months. Include key dates, costs, sales goals, etc.

Product 1 _____

Product 2 _____

Product 3 _____

Product 4 _____

Define the impact a new product/service might have on other products or services you offer. _____

_____

_____

How will the products complement other products/services in the product line?

_____

_____

_____

What other currently offered products/services can be used with this product?

_____

_____

_____

Identify and describe the risks associated with your product/service. _____

_____

_____

_____

How will the product be sold? List all distribution channels including additional staffing and training that may be needed. _____

_____

_____

Explain how the product/service relates to the mission and strategic direction of your company. _____

_____

_____

Detail all promotions planned for the year—by month, quantity, costs and expected response and sales.

Promotion	Month	Expected Costs	Expected Response	Projected Sales

List the demographic, psychographic and geographic traits of the ideal customer.

Demographic	Psychographic	Geographic

Summarize your pricing strategy. Describe:

Special offer pricing:_____

_____

_____

Introductory pricing: _____

_____

_____

Multiple discount pricing: _____

_____

_____

Wholesale pricing: _____

_____

_____

Provide a descriptive statement on how the sales are to be achieved.

- Include as much detail as possible as well as a timetable.
- Review your distribution, sales responsibilities, monitoring and sales strategies.

Spread expected sales and costs by month for the year ahead. The budget will relate directly to advertising and other promotions.

Include an estimated P&L calculation for each promotion planned. Use the P&L worksheet provided in this chapter.

Remember to Register

In order to gain access to free forms, dictionaries, checklists and updates, readers must register their book purchase at <u>Socrates.com</u>. An eight-digit Registration Code is provided on the enclosed CD. See page iv for further details.

Section ■ Three

7 Turning on Sales

Overview

How will the customer buy your product or service? Is it better to pay commissions to independent sales representatives or create an in-house sales team? Carefully consider all your options before committing time and resources to creating an in-house sales team. There are advantages and disadvantages associated with both kinds of reps. When addressing the sales portion of your marketing strategy, consider the following points:

Organization

- Do you intend to use an internal or external sales force?

- Is your product/service line split by type of product/service, geographical area or specialty?

- What are your other levels of distribution: distributors, dealers, manufacturers' representatives, franchising, multilevel sales, direct sales?

- If building an in-house sales force, will you have floor persons, telemarketing, sales managers?

- If using an outside sales force, are there representatives who call on customers or sell in their office or showroom? Will they exhibit at trade shows? Who will pay for their travel and time? What expenses will you reimburse?

- If using outside sales reps, how do you qualify and select them?

- Does the actual sales activity take place in your place of business or the customer's house, office or plant?

- Are salespeople supported by salaries, salary plus commission, commission only, draw and commission, bonuses or independent contractors? Do commission amounts vary by product? What incentives will you award?

- Will you provide sales training in the form of seminars, online classes, books, tapes, etc.?

- Who will supervise the salespeople?

Sales Volume

- What are your daily, weekly, monthly and yearly sales goals?
- What are your sales per person goals?
- What is the average number of contacts you need to close a sale?
- Who is responsible for obtaining the credit check?
- Who is responsible for overseeing the fulfillment of all orders once the order has been placed?
- What is your cost of sales? (Cost of sales is determined by dividing the costs associated with acquiring a customer by the gross unit sale.)
- How will you break sales territories into regions or states? (Chart in map form.)
- Who determines the sales goal for each rep?

Product Line	Sales Goals	Sales per Person Goals	Average No. of Contacts Needed to Close a Sale	Cost of Sales
Product A	Daily	Rep 1		
	Weekly	Rep 2		
	Monthly	Rep 3	5	
	Yearly	Rep 4		
		Rep 5		
		Other		
Product B	Daily	Rep 1		
	Weekly	Other	2	
	Monthly			
	Yearly			
Service A	Daily	Rep 1		
	Weekly	Rep 2	6	
	Monthly	Other		
	Yearly			

Distribution

- How is your product shipped?
- Who pays the shipping costs?
- What is the average shipping length?

Your choice of distribution channel has a direct impact on your contact with your customer, your profit margin and delivery time. The distribution channels you use to deliver your product or service into the hands of your customers affects the markup and profit margin you can expect.

Markup is added to the cost of your product. It is a percentage increase you add to the cost of the product or service to arrive at the price you charge to the customer. A 100 percent markup means the customer will pay twice the actual cost of the product or service.

Sales Forecasting

Estimating sales potential can be a hit-or-miss proposition. One method of accurately forecasting sales is to calculate the total sales potential for your market, then estimate the percentage of that market you believe you can capture. The total sales potential for a market is the total amount of the products or services currently being sold by all your competitors in your market. An accurate sales forecast will help you achieve the following aspects of your business plan:

- determining markets for your products and services
- planing and implementing business strategies
- developing sales quotas
- determining whether and how many salespeople are needed
- deciding on distribution channels and alternatives
- developing pricing strategies for products and services
- analyzing new product and service offerings
- calculating total profit and sales potential
- creating advertising alternatives and promotion budgets

Learning the Language of Business

Readers are entitled to full access and use of the comprehensive Business Law and Accounting & Finance Dictionaries found on the Web landing page at www.socrates.com/books/business-plan.aspx. Please remember to register the first time you use this free resource. See page iv for instructions.

Product Line	Markets Defined— Estimated Sales Potential per Year	Sales Quotas	Number of Salespeople Needed to Reach Sales Goal	Distribution Channels	Pricing Strategy	Total Sales Profit and Potential	Advertising Alternatives and Promotion Budgets
Product A	$2.3 million	50% of total sales or $1.15 million	5	Marketing, wholesale, retail, direct to customer, sales reps	Maintain current pricing structure Offer preferred customer pricing	20% profit margin anticipated	Support sales with brochures, space ads, fliers to consumer.
Product B	$50,000	$10,000	1	Retail, wholesale, direct to customer	Maintain current pricing	10% profit margin anticipated	Place two ads per year
Service A	$500,000	$500,000	2	Sales reps	Offer introductory pricing—first 6 months	35% profit margin anticipated	Send mailing to current customer base

Forecasted Sales by Sales Representative by Month

Product Line	Product A—$1.5 million					Product B—$10,000	Product C—$500,000	
	Sales Rep 1	Sales Rep 2	Sales Rep 3	Sales Rep 4	Sales Rep 5	Sales Rep 1	Sales Rep 1	Sales Rep 2
January	$25,000	$25,000	$25,000	$25,000	$25,000	$5,000	$25,000	$15,000
February	$50,000	$50,000	$50,000	$50,000	$50,000	$0	$10,000	$35,000
March	$25,000	$25,000	$25,000	$25,000	$25,000	$0	$10,000	$35,000
April	$25,000	$25,000	$25,000	$25,000	$25,000	$0	$10,000	$25,000
May	$25,000	$25,000	$25,000	$25,000	$25,000	$0	$10,000	$25,000
June	$25,000	$25,000	$25,000	$25,000	$25,000	$0	$25,000	$25,000
July	$0	$0	$0	$0	$0	$0	$25,000	$25,000
August	$25,000	$25,000	$25,000	$25,000	$25,000	$0	$25,000	$10,000
September	$50,000	$50,000	$50,000	$50,000	$50,000	$0	$25,000	$10,000
October	$25,000	$25,000	$25,000	$25,000	$25,000	$0	$35,000	$10,000
November	$25,000	$25,000	$25,000	$25,000	$25,000	$0	$35,000	$10,000
December	$0	$0	$0	$0	$0	$5,000	$15,000	$25,000
Total	$300,000	$300,000	$300,000	$300,000	$300,000	$10,000	$250,000	$250,000

A blank Forecasted Sales by Sales Representative by Month is also available in Chapter 20: Planning Worksheets.

Building a Sales Team

Building an Internal Team versus Outsourcing

Which is right for your business? Building an in-house sales team or outsourcing sales reps? Both structures have their advantages and drawbacks. Weigh the pros and cons of each.

In-House Sales Force

The term in-house refers to an individual or team of sales representatives who are employees of a company and sell the company's products only. The sales representatives are hired by the company and are trained and compensated by the company.

Advantages

You can exert 100 percent control over your internal sales force by deciding which products they push, how much time is spent on each product and who they call.

Disadvantages

You absorb 100 percent of the costs associated with their sales efforts. In order to make a salesperson's time profitable to the company, you must be able to find enough sales potential within any given geographical area or target market to sustain the costs associated with their efforts.

Manufacturers' Reps

Manufacturers' reps, also known as independent agents, are independent salespeople who represent more than one company's products. They are paid a commission from every sale they make. The collection of products they choose to sell is usually directed to a specific industry or market. The companies the salespeople represent are usually noncompetitive, but complement each other. The amount of commission you award for each sale may vary with the product sold and the sales amount. Some sales reps are part of a larger rep agency, while others work on their own as independents.

Advantages

Utilizing manufacturers' reps will help keep your costs down, for they can cover a wide geographical area for minimal expense. You do not have the out-of-pocket expense of maintaining an internal sales force: no salaries, benefits or travel expenses.

Disadvantages

You cannot mandate the amount of time or effort an independent rep will spend selling your products or services. In order to cover a wider geographic area, you may need to hire a number of independent reps to cover your selected territories. That will mean additional training and high levels of management to oversee each group. Finally, if a rep drops another company's product line that complements your offerings, you may lose valuable synergies.

To know if you should hire inside sales or independent reps, follow these guidelines:

- If you have an easy product or service to sell with limited finances, consider hiring independent reps.
- If your products are complicated or difficult to sell but you are adequately financed, consider hiring your own in-house sales team.
- If you sell a small-ticket item throughout a wide territory, consider hiring independent reps.
- If you sell a big-ticket item within a small territory, consider hiring your own in-house sales team.

Pulling It All Together

Include the following information in your business plan:

1. Describe the organization of your sales team.

2. Explain the reasons for selecting an internal or external sales force.

3. Describe your different levels of distribution.

4. Outline how sales personnel will be paid.

5. Describe your training programs for sales personnel—both face to face and telesales reps.

6. Explain who on your management team will be responsible for the sales team.

7. Include your sales team's goals by month.

8. Explain how you divided up reps by territory.

8 Growth Profitability with Product Development

Overview

Most businesses are created with a specific product or service in mind, but sometimes the development of a new product of service just evolves. New product ideas come from just about anywhere—a vendor, a trade publication, employees and competitors. In fact, the overwhelming majority of ideas will come from your customers. Listen carefully to customer comments, written evaluations and inquiries about other products and services you may offer.

Every product goes through a life cycle from inception to discontinued use. The four stages of a life cycle include:

Market Development–new product or service is introduced to the market. At this point sales are slow as customers are unfamiliar with the product.

Market Growth–Sales steadily increase as a general awareness of the product improves. At this point, competition will begin to pop up.

Maturity—Overall demand begins to level off as competition increases.

Market Decline–Customer demand for the product or service begins to decline as new technology and improved variations of the product introduced by other companies make your product obsolete.

"The risk taking occurs at the beginning of the building process. I am building a product for a customer that will hopefully appreciate it and pay for it, but I may not be sure anyone will buy it. Just in case, I will conduct a considerable number of online surveys, focus groups and have constant customer contact trying to listen to where the market is for what we are doing. The truth is, even if we get it absolutely right, we are going to be wrong 20 percent of the time, and if we did that successfully, it is going to make us phenomenally successful."

William Lederer, Chairman & CEO
Minotaur Capital Management
Chicago, IL

Growth Plan

Review your ideas on a regular basis—once a month, quarterly, semiannually or annually. Include in your planning process a dedicated time to review new ideas.

Different growth strategies may be developed to grow your company sales.

Same Product—Same Market

Encourage people to use your product more by developing new uses for the product. Encourage greater product use—increase demand by encouraging customers to increase consumption of your product or service. This can be achieved through increasing quantities sold, offering volume discounts for higher unit sales or packaging two or more products together to increase the unit sale and winning over your competitor's customers.

New Market—Same Product

Find new markets for your existing product by reaching out to a completely new audience or geographic area.

New Product—Same Market

Include new product features, options or complementary products or services to your current product offering. You can expand your product or service two ways: offering new features or creating related or spinoff families of products.

New Market—New Product

Grow your business by diversifying your company offering. This growth plan is recommended only after you have exhausted all other growth strategies. Gaining entry into a new market can be achieved by leveraging off your company name to introduce new products in new markets.

All new products follow a development process. A typical development process may look like this:

1. **Develop an Idea.** Ideas come from a variety of sources. When an idea hits, write it down for further evaluation or file it away for future consideration.

2. **Evaluate the Idea.** Together with the individuals responsible for product development, evaluate each idea for profit potential, ease of manufacturing, competition and pricing.

   Thoroughly investigate each idea by asking yourself the following:

   - Do you have the cash to back the idea?
   - Do you have the staff to develop and sell the idea?
   - Is a comparable product already being offered by a competitor? If yes, how is your idea better than or unique to what they offer?
   - What void is your product or service filling that your competitor's is not?
   - What is the potential market universe?
   - Does the idea fit with your mission statement?
   - What will this product cost to produce?

> **Hint**
>
> If you cannot answer each question with a positive answer or unique positioning, rethink the idea. It is an expensive proposition to develop new products and before you expend limited resources developing a weak product, it is always smarter to cut your losses before getting too emotionally involved with an idea.

3. **Analyze Your Opportunity.** Conduct an informal focus group with a small group of current customers. Select a group of customers similar to your target market and ask them to evaluate the idea. Their comments and suggestions may help you create a product or service that is better than your original idea.

4. **Develop Your Product.** Once you have thoroughly evaluated the idea and have received positive customer feedback, develop the product or service.

5. **Test the Market.** Develop a prototype or conduct a beta test with a small group of customers. This will help you work out any bugs and will serve as a preliminary to introducing it to the general market.

6. **Introduce the Product or Service to the Marketplace.** If you make it through steps 1–5, it is time to roll your product out to the marketplace.

Product Development Checklist

Product: _____

Projected ship date: _____

Initial production quantity: _____

1. Production

Design specifications: _____

Materials required: _____

Employee hours required: _____

Temporary help required: _____

Equipment required: _____

2. Miscellaneous Production

Storage requirements: _____

Other packaging: _____

3. Other Costs

Licensing fees: _____

4. Order Entry

Pricing discounts: _____

Shipping schedules: _____

Distribution: _____

5. Marketing

Marketing research: _____

Marketing plan: _____

Pricing: _____

Methods: _____

Stuffers: _____

Direct mail: _____

Telemarketing: _____

Sales reps: _____

Trade show: _____

PR: _____

Customer service: _____

Packaging with other products: _____

6. General

Set sales goals: _____

Determine costs: _____

Calculate break-even: _____

Development Timeline

Product Development Sales and Costs Forecast

An important factor to consider before bringing any product to market is determining if the new product or service will make money. Sales are very difficult to project for any new product, and costs may be difficult to separate out, but a rough sales/expense estimate is necessary to decide if the project has enough merit to move forward.

This worksheet will help you estimate product development sales and costs for the next 3 years.

Product Development Sales/Cost Forecast			
Product:			
Sales	Year One	Year Two	Year Three
Total Market–Available Universe:			
Expected Percentage of Market We Will Gain:			
Projected Number of Units/Orders Placed:			
Selling Price (per Unit/per Sale)			
Gross Sales Volume Anticipated:			
Total Sales Revenues Anticipated:			

Costs	Year One—Initial Development Costs	Ongoing Development Costs
Cost of Goods Sold		
Materials + 10 percent		
Direct Labor		
Research & Development		
Sales & Marketing		
Overhead		
Indirect Labor		
Overhead Allocation (20–25 percent of each sale)		
Total Expenses		
Total Revenues		
Total Expenses		
(Subtract Total Revenues From Total Expenses)		

Sample Product Development Plan

A Sample Product Development Plan begins on the next page.

Pulling It All Together

Describe your core products and any unique features.

_____

_____

_____

_____

Looking at your core product list is there a spinoff product idea that can be explored? What is it?

_____

_____

_____

_____

Detail your plan to grow sales of your products or services.

_____

_____

_____

_____

Product Acquisition

Identify any products or services already offered by competitors that would make prime acquisition targets.

_____

_____

_____

_____

List all reasons why a competitor's product or service may be a good fit with your current product or service offering.

_____

_____

_____

_____

VisualKeeper

Project: VisualKeeper (for Content)

Product Development Proposal

Creation Date:

Document Owner:

Last Update:

VisualKeeper (for Content)

Product Concept and Preliminary Market Identification

Companies struggle to keep up with technology and the demand for more storage capabilities to house their electronic data. Companies spend huge amounts of time and resources each year to create electronic images, lists and text. Electronic marketing is being incorporated into more marketing programs. Once the documents are created, the issue becomes where to store all this electronic material.

The typical company stores departmental materials on individuals' computers. The art department stores their creations on CDs or on their desktops. The marketing department will keep pertinent documents on the originator's computer or on disks. Many nontech companies do not maintain corporate Intranets for centralized storage. The danger to individual document storage is losing materials when the document holder leaves the company, a computer crashes or a disk goes bad. Plus, no matter how documents are created and named, someone is responsible for remembering where it is, which version is the most recent and what it is named.

The Current Product

VisualKeeper is Company A's solution to the hassles associated with content management. VisualKeeper organizes and stores documents in one location for easy uploading, retrieval, sending, updating and organizing.

Material or content is stored in a custom database. The database is secure and the client controls access to its images. Those with permission can use any of the multiple search options available to locate content quickly, import or export files, update materials or e-mail materials in a matter of seconds.

When Company A's VisualKeeper is coupled with Distributor A's InstantContent, images are served from Company A's servers to multiple locations. End users are provided with faster downloads and consistent delivery of graphic files, music, video and content.

Using one central location to store electronic content helps companies manage and maintain corporate materials with ease. Sending materials to promotional agencies, updating images and maintaining organized files are easy with VisualKeeper.

Because VisualKeeper is Internet-based, it is easily accessible with just a URL, username and password, from anywhere at any time. With a few simple clicks of the mouse, access can be granted or denied depending on project or personnel changes. With VisualKeeper, designers, off-site employees, content providers, copywriters, suppliers and virtually anyone else who needs to access a client's content is able to do so, and multiple people can access VisualKeeper simultaneously. VisualKeeper's search function makes finding content easy, no matter how many thousands of files are stored. Conduct a standard or advanced search by keyword, categories, caption heading, byline or photographer.

VisualKeeper frees up valuable server space. Content will never be lost due to server failure or corrupted disks. Files are hosted, stored and backed up on Company A's secure network.

VisualKeeper is written to accept images only—streaming media and flash documents.

VisualKeeper has been built as a stand alone image storage management system. We partnered with Distributor A to serve Supplier A's images and for Distributor A to absorb the high-volume Web traffic Supplier A's mailings create. It is important to note that Company A has the storage and equipment capability to maintain and serve images and is therefore not reliant on Distributor A's technology or equipment. The Distributor A and Company A process works as follows: When a Supplier A customer clicks on an image link, the image request is registered by Distributor A. If Distributor A does not have the image on its servers, it comes to Company A to retrieve the stored image and place it on their server closest in proximity to the customer's geographic location.

The Benefits of VisualKeeper in its Current Form

- VisualKeeper is a stand-alone image storage management system.
- VisualKeeper is Internet based; it is easily accessible with just a URL.
- Access to VisualKeeper can be turned on or off based on individual needs.
- VisualKeeper frees up valuable server space.
- Content maintained will never be lost due to server failure or corrupted disks.
- VisualKeeper is a load balancing system that manages high-volume Internet image traffic without the fear of overloading or crashing a company server.

Product Concept Description

Historical Perspective

VisualKeeper is a content management database that allows clients to store an unlimited number of images on Company A's servers, and through the power of a partnership, Distributor A's InstantContent serves up those images. This powerful combination enhances end-user experience while eliminating strain on or the need to purchase additional infrastructure.

VisualKeeper has not been actively promoted by sales or account management (AM) teams. It was introduced to the sales team in late October, early November. Company A teamed with Distributor A to create an image storage system (Company A) and an image distribution tool. When a customer clicks or calls up the image from VisualKeeper, Distributor As' InstantContent, a powerful Internet content distribution tool sends the image to Web sites via worldwide content access points. Content is distributed more efficiently and cost-effectively than the original server.

During the past 2 months VisualKeeper has been undergoing a name change and other quick fixes. The product is scheduled to be reintroduced, in its current form, to the sales and AM teams during the month of January.

The benefits of VisualKeeper are that VisualKeeper helps companies save money by maintaining and managing all images in one location—lowering infrastructure costs, increasing time to market and assuring that materials are safe from damage, corruption and loss.

VisualKeeper was created at the request of a Company A CRM customer, Supplier A. VisualKeeper is being used by Supplier A to balance its server loads during peak mailing times.

Proposed Product Expansion

VisualKeeper provides a solution to companies that lack the capability to handle high-volume Internet traffic or simply do not have enough corporate storage space to maintain and organize company documents.

The proposed product change is to expand VisualKeeper's current capabilities to accept not only images but other content forms such as lists, text and HTML documents, PDFs, etc. VisualKeeper will be a promoted as a total document storage and management system. In addition to uploading images, clients will be able to upload text and HTML documents, PDFs, e-mail messages, lists, banner ads, etc.

Files will be stored in one account, separated by document type—e.g., image, list, document, PDF, e-mail message, banner ad.

The main menu will be expanded to allow the user the ability to search for a document format.

Security may be changed to allow specific users image-only security or access to a combination of formats—i.e., images, PDFs, e-mail messages and banner ads. Other individuals may have access to images, e-mail messages and lists only.

In the future, Company A may consider providing additional storage capabilities to Company A members at a comparable price of $3.95 per month.

Search Tool

A comprehensive search tool will assist users in locating files. The search tool can be used to locate a file by keywords, heading, caption, bylines or photographer.

Remember to Register

In order to gain access to free forms, dictionaries, checklists and updates, readers must register their book purchase at Socrates.com. An eight-digit Registration Code is provided on the enclosed CD. See page iv for further details.

In addition to the current search capabilities the search, function will be expanded to include:

- Articles: last date published

                    locate articles that have been used fewer than XX times or more than XX times

                    author name

                    publication

                    title

- Lists: last update

                    name

- E-mail Messages: text

                    HTML

- Documents: PDF

                    text

                    HTML

- Ads   space or banner

Upload Features

Mass image imports require Company A's intervention. This bulk method of importing images will not change.

Currently, individual document uploads can be done by users using the upload feature. We will continue to offer this method of importing one document at a time but will designate the import by type of document. When importing a single document, users will identify the type of document—prior to browsing and uploading the document.

- List
- Document
- Banner Ads
- Image
- E-mail Messages

Editing Features

Currently, editing of image information can be done in real time by clicking on the search link, then clicking the Edit button to make changes to image information—caption, byline, etc.

Changes to the actual image cannot be done in real time and can only by done by first deleting the old image and uploading the new image or, by directly uploading the new image to replace the obsolete image.

The edit feature will be made consistent for all images and documents. The update document protection safeguards will remain as is. If a user wishes to make changes to a document, the original document must be deleted and replaced with a new document, or a new document can be uploaded to overwrite the original document. It is important to note that once the original document is updated with a newer, edited version, the original version cannot be retrieved.

Various user security accesses will be granted in order for individuals to search, send, edit, upload or delete documents.

Reporting Tools

New reporting tools will be created to provide companies with a snapshot of who is visiting their site, through which access points and time stamps.

Reporting information includes summary logs containing information about:

- who is viewing content—user access;
- listing of access points—by user and time stamp; and
- total volume of traffic accessing content—weekly and monthly counts.

Partnering With Distributor A

Company A has a 12-month partnership agreement with Distributor A. The agreement is up for renewal in August 20XX. The partnership works.

Options

1. We can renew our partnership agreement with Distributor A as an Internet image content distribution partner. Distributor A will continue to serve images to the distribution point nearest the requestor's location.

2. We could consider Distributor A a competitor and discontinue our partnership agreement when it expires in August, realizing that we will eventually be a serious player in the image storage and serving market.

Recommendation

I recommend maintaining the partnership. Although VisualKeeper has been created as a stand-alone image storage management and distribution system and is not dependent on Distributor A to store, manage or distribute images, I recommend that Company A continue the current partnership with Distributor A for at least 12, but not more than 24 months. Once we establish a solid customer base for VisualKeeper, we can then discontinue the partnership with Distributor A and promote VisualKeeper as a stand-alone competing product.

Maintaining a partnership with Distributor A as we launch this product is beneficial to Company A in the following ways:

- Company A can capitalize on the strength of Distributor A's promotional branding.
- Company A's partnering with Distributor A lends credibility to VisualKeeper.

Current Uses of This Product

VisualKeeper eliminates many of the hassles associated with image storage management as well as production issues that may arise. The system enables a company to efficiently manage all of its images in one place. Maintaining one database of images makes it easier for companies to control which image version is utilized in their promotions, ensuring that images will be consistent throughout all promotions regardless of the agencies or designers involved.

Clients control who can have access to their repository. Security can be granted or denied quickly and easily. Additionally, there is no limit to the number of people who can access the same repository simultaneously—meaning that every authorized user from a company could access its database at the same time.

Balances Server Loads

VisualKeeper allows clients to store images on Company A's servers while Distributor A's InstaContent serves up those images. This powerful combination enhances end-user experience while eliminating strain on or the need to purchase additional infrastructure. When a customer clicks or calls up an image, the image is served from VisualKeeper. Content is served more efficiently and cost-effectively. Slowdowns and delays caused by heavy Internet traffic to the client's site are eliminated, keeping their systems running smoothly and evenly.

Image Management

As an image management tool, VisualKeeper can store an unlimited number of images, providing companies a single source location for all their images. Locating images is easy when using the keyword, category, byline, author name, word contains, etc., search features. Importing images is easy with the upload retrieval system. Revised images can be imported to replace obsolete images at a moment's notice. There is no worry about cycle updates or lag time before an image is accessible; updates are on real time.

Flash and streaming media content can be stored and distributed by VisualKeeper as well.

Benefits of This Product to Our Customers and to Company A:

Strategic Fit

This is a natural extension of our current product offering. VisualKeeper is currently being offered to Company A clients as an image management system.

- Expanding the capabilities of VisualKeeper to our current clients will benefit them with additional storage options at a minimal cost.

- Prospects that may not be immediately interested in our other services may be interested in our storage capacity. Gaining new VisualKeeper clients will keep our product and company name visible.

- Creating a trusting relationship with our VisualKeeper clients may generate additional sales in the future.

- VisualKeeper as a supplement product to our core business will generate a consistent and dependable revenue stream based on annual contracts.

- Company A has the storage capacity and equipment to provide companies a quick and easy way to keep track of all their electronic materials.

- We have an extensive list of past clients to whom we can remarket this new product.

- Introducing VisualKeeper provides an excellent opportunity to create new clients and to create awareness of Company A's products and services.

Impact on Other Company A Products

- VisualKeeper will attract new customers to Company A who, in turn, will become aware of Company A's other products and services.

- PR gained from VisualKeeper will create additional awareness of Company A's technological abilities.

- VisualKeeper, with its annual commitment and monthly fee structure, will produce a predictable revenue source for Company A. Where our core product relies heavily on seasonality, VisualKeeper will produce a set amount of revenue each month.

Market Definitions

Competition

> **Competitors are divided into two distinct categories that target two distinct audiences:**
>
> **1. Direct competitors**–offering image storage and distribution systems include: Distributors A, B and C. These companies promote their services to the business market. A fourth competitor ceased operations.
>
> **2 Indirect competitors**–offering image and document storage without the sophisticated distribution capabilities (include a number of other named companies). These companies are promoting their services directly to the consumer market and offer storage space for e-mails, documents, photos, etc. Purchasing additional storage space with some of these companies typically costs from $3.95/month for up to 2GB of storage space to $9.95/month for 150MB of storage space.

> **Note**
>
> Another supplier is attempting to capture both the consumer and business market. Their monthly charge for basic storage services range from $3.95 ($42 annually) for 2GB of storage all the way up to $34.95 ($369 annually) for 2,000GB of storage.

A full competitive overview of each company's service and capabilities is attached.

Why Will This Product be Used Over Our Competitors?

- Company A's commitment and reliability within the technology sector.

- Clients who purchase repeatedly with Company A will enjoy the convenience of having all their e-mail messages, in house fliers and banner ads in one location.

- Competitors offer image storage services. Company A will be the only image storage system that will allow storage of image and nonimage files

Hurdles

- Our three main competitors' main product is image storage and distribution. Company A will be offering VisualKeeper as an add-on product. However, this product could become a significant revenue producer if a strong sales push is behind the product.

- Distributor A, Distributor B and Distributor C have been offering image storage and distribution longer than Company A.

- Companies are scaling back on their outside expenses. For example, Supplier A is considering discontinuing using VisualKeeper and bringing its image management in-house to cut costs and save money.

- Companies may not have need for an outside storage/management system. It is common for companies to develop a corporate Intranet system with public folders that employees may access with security clearance.

Technology Hurdles

VisualKeeper is currently written in Linux. We do not have the knowledge or means to support a Linux product other than light triage. We are a Windows® shop. A full rewrite is required to convert the VisualKeeper to a Windows format. Estimated time needed to rewrite program is one SE developer for 2 full weeks (estimated cost: $16,.000).

Despite the rumors that 4 terabytes of memory is available in our San Francisco location, it does not mean there is that much storage capacity available to dedicate to VisualKeeper. It is true that our San Francisco site does have a lot of equipment, but they do not have the storage capacity. According to our technology employees, our San Francisco office has 4 terabytes of storage. There are 2½ terabytes currently being used, leaving a balance of 1½ terabytes available—but not necessarily storage space. Plus, they have six connections and all six are being used. To create more connections, we will need to purchase approximately $40,000 worth of equipment. Our tech group stated it would be more costly to attach our VisualKeeper to their systems than to rewrite it and keep it here (mostly because we do not have the knowledge to support the program in its current Linux form).

Additional Equipment Requirements

We have the computer capability we need to expand VisualKeeper but not the storage capacity. The purchase of new disks to create 250 gigabytes of expandable storage will be necessary at an approximate cost of $10,000.

Target Audience

The target audience consists of smaller nontech companies that may not have technological resources or storage capabilities:

- Publishing companies–Publishers could be a primary target industry and have the greatest number of applications for VisualKeeper. Publishing companies are notorious for creating volumes of content with nowhere to house or retrieve it. The old publishing adage, Content is King, is true. From repurposing content, licensing content, archiving book text, storing marketing collateral and maintaining author photos, publishers succeed or fail based on how they utilize published text.

- Advertising agencies–This can be an added service ad agencies provide to their clients. Agencies will be able to store all their clients' images and materials in VisualKeeper for quick retrieval.

- Corporations with multiple branches of offices–Headquartered companies need to provide consistent image and collateral documentation to all their offices. VisualKeeper is the one location that users can access to retrieve corporate materials.

- Direct marketers who maintain their own lists–Any company that collects and markets to multiple or specialized e-mail addresses can maintain individual files in VisualKeeper. High-volume direct marketers and e-mail marketers will be able to utilize VisualKeeper to organize their e-mail messages, banner ads and all their marketing collateral in one location.

- Catalogers who e-mail catalogs or manage thousands of product images and print and electronic advertising–including space ads and banner ads–will also be able to utilize VisualKeeper.

As indicated by the competitive analysis, large Fortune 1000 companies also utilize image storage and distribution systems.

Niche markets may include packaged goods companies, hotel chains, catalogers, financial services, insurance companies, retailers, etc. The ideal market to go after is the established brick and mortar companies who typically generate excessive amounts of paper/electronic documents that need to be saved or stored.

Who Will be the Decision Maker?

The decision to purchase and implement VisualKeeper can rest with company presidents, information technology directors, database administrators, marketing directors, vice presidents, agency principals, chief operating officers, chief executive officers, chief financial officers and agency directors.

Support

- Company A sales–to sell the product to current and prospective clients

- Company A marketing–to provide marketing support, press releases, collateral and trade show exposure.

- Company A campaign and account managers–to suggest to current clients and include in prospect proposals as a storage management and document retrieval system.

Preliminary Product Team

Development

The product development team will create specs, test completed product, train users, launch product, provide ongoing support and provide demonstrations to clients and Company A employees as needed.

Marketing

The marketing team will assist with sales collateral creation, marketing promotions and press promotion (PR).

Sales and Account Management (AM) Teams

The Sales and AM teams will promote VisualKeeper to new and prospective clients.

Information Technology

The information technology team will handle equipment and maintenance.

Software Engineers (SE)

The SE team will rewrite and maintain product.

Pricing

Pricing will remain consistent with current VisualKeeper pricing structure:

- There will be an initial, one-time setup fee of $1,000 per repository.

- A $250 monthly charge per account up to 2 gigabytes (2 million kilobytes) of storage space will apply.

- Additional storage space can be purchased at $200 for each additional 2-gig increment of storage space used beyond the initial 2 gigs—gigs 3-4, 5-6, etc.

- A monthly $18 per gig delivery charge will apply. Charges will be variable based on the total image size delivered each month.

- A 12-month minimum contract will be required.

Financials

Estimated number of clients signed on first 6 months:		
12 new clients with minimum 2 gigs of storage		
Projected revenues for first 6 months:		
$12,000 setup fee (12 clients × $1,000 one-time setup fee)		
Monthly charges:	3 clients × 3 months @ $250 =	$2,250
	3 clients × 4 months @ $250 =	$3,000
	6 clients × 2 months @ $250 =	$3,000
Delivery charges:	3 clients × 3 months @ $54 =	$486
	3 clients × 4 months @ $54 =	$648
	6 clients × 2 months @ $54 =	$648
	Subtotal	**$10,032**
Projected revenues for second 6 months:		
$12,000 setup fee (12 clients × $1,000 one-time setup fee)		
Monthly charges:	15 clients × 6 months @ $250 =	$ 22,500
	18 clients × 4 months @ $250 =	$18,000
	24 clients × 2 months @ $250 =	$12,000
Delivery charges:	15 clients × 6 months @ $54 =	$4,860
	18 clients × 4 months @ $54 =	$3,888
	24 clients × 2 months @ $54 =	$2,592
	Subtotal	**$63,840**
	First year total:	**$73,872**

* Company A will charge the client a $27/gig delivery fee. Currently we are charged $18/gig image delivery fee by Distributor A, giving Company A a net profit of $9 per gig delivered. If we discontinue our partnership with Distributor A to deliver content these charges will disappear.

Equipment Costs:	
Development costs @ $200/hour × 80 hours	= $16,000
Equipment costs (disks)	= $10,000
Equipment subtotal:	**$26,000**

Selling/Maintenance Costs	
Monthly commitment charges from **Distributor A** @ $2,000/mo	= $24,000
Sales commissions to reps (15 percent)	= $10,700
Marketing: writing costs, staff costs	= $ 3,000
Creative: market collateral design costs	= $ 2,500
Ongoing maintenance costs	= $ 5,000
Overhead (20 percent)	= $14,000
Salaries (25 percent of revenues)	= $15,000
Anticipated costs less equipment:	$74,200
Projected year 1 net profit:	<$328>
Year 2	
Sales:	= $150,000
Costs:	= $117,000
Projected year 2 net profit:	**$ 33,000**

The key to making this product profitable will be to sign up a minimum of five clients at a flat monthly fee of $3,000 or sign up 50 clients at a recurring monthly charge of $250/month plus distribution fees.

Historical Revenues

Company A charges Supplier A $3,000/month for VisualKeeper/Distributor A storage and distribution services. (We do not charge extra delivery charges.) Distributor A charges Company A $2,000/month commitment fee. Distributor A serves up an average of 14 million Supplier A images monthly at an average size of 3k per image. Delivery charges–if billed by Distributor A–would be $27 per gig or $1,134/monthly delivery charges.

Backup

Backup procedures will be conducted consistent with Company A's security policies.

How the Screen Will Look

The screen will look like the VisualKeeper screen but will be expanded to include options to view by account:

• lists	• images	• articles
• e-mail messages	• PDFs	• banner/space ads

Lists can be uploaded the same as images—via the browse function. The client will be able to e-mail the list in VisualKeeper for editing. Once the file is edited, it can be uploaded back into the VisualKeeper database.

Additional Research

- Survey to existing customers about their current and future storage capabilities.

- Request additional information from the sales/AM teams.

- Talk directly to current and past clients regarding their needs.

- Contact other companies, including Company B and Company C. These companies publish paid subscription magazines and newsletters. Both companies are smaller with approximately 25 to 75 employees on staff. They have limited infrastructure and resources.

- Work with sales—Sales Rep A (East Coast sales rep) is currently working with our clients. She has e-mailed them to discuss their current and future needs for a storage management and delivery system. She has a conference call scheduled with a prospect company and will discuss it with them during the call. Ask the other members of the sales team their clients' storage/distribution plans for the next 12 months.

- Work with AMs—AM A is working with Supplier A. He will ask them this week about their usage of VisualKeeper and other potential uses of the product for their marketing plans.

- Work with marketing to create a questionnaire regarding customer storage capabilities, now and in the future.

- Work with Software Engineers—rewriting VisualKeeper from a Linux format to a Windows format will take approximately one week for one engineer. The system should be completely rewritten to accommodate the inclusion of nonimage documents.

Distribution of Data: E-mailing Documents to Recipients

VisualKeeper provides users the ability to e-mail documents to recipients for easy distribution.

Documents may be sent to an individual for read-only purposes or for editing. Once a document is uploaded into VisualKeeper, it remains in the format in which it was uploaded. For instance, if an image is uploaded into VisualKeeper as low resolution, it cannot be changed into a high-resolution image. If an article was uploaded as a PDF, it will remain as a PDF in VisualKeeper. If an e-mail message was uploaded in HTML, it will not be convertible to a text format.

Data Formats

- lists–sent in CSV format

- images–viewable only

- articles–sent in either HTML or text format; may be read as a WordPad, Word document, etc.

- e-mail messages–sent in either HTML or text format; depends on how the file was saved in VisualKeeper

- PDFs–will always remain as a pdf file

- banner/space ads–will remain in format in which they were uploaded

Estimated Time from Creation to Launch

- proposed launch date: to be determined with marketing
- develop product: 1 week
- testing: 1 week
- move from development server to live server: 1 day
- retesting: ½ day
- create marketing collateral: 2 weeks
- launch product: 1 week

Product Rollout Process

See attached sheet.

What Will the Product Look Like?

See attached PowerPoint screens.

Product Rollout Process for VisualKeeper for Content

Product:	VisualKeeper for Content
This product originates:	Internally with partnership with Distributor A
Product manager:	(This person is ultimately responsible for the complete rollout of this product, which includes ensuring the completion of all of the tasks below—including that a person and department are assigned to each and that a due date is assigned)
Product sponsor:	
Internal product rollout date:	
External product rollout date:	

Task (if not applicable, write N/A through)	Department Responsible	Person Responsible	Due Date
Name of product	Marketing/Product Development		
Determine if this product is filling a hole in the current product offering (based on feedback from the market); is an enhancement to an existing product; complement to an existing product; or is an introduction of a whole new product line.	Product Development		
How is it packaged—Quantity sold? Per thousand?	Product Development		
Pricing determined	Product Development		
How will we monetize this?			
Volume discount			
New rate card created or existing rate card adjusted?	Product Development		
Updates in future	Sales/Finance		
Execution process	Information Technology, Marketing, Sales, Operations		
Who is involved?			
What tools do they need?			
Technology adjusted to accommodate	Information Technology		
Determine commission rate paid to sales reps	Sales		
Incentive program attached to first sales of this product	Sales		
External promotion plan for this new product	Product development/Marketing	Product Development/ Marketing Specialist A	
Press release	Marketing		

Letter for sales to send out to clients/prospects	Product Development
Attachment/samples/demos to send to clients/prospects	Product Development
Slides for sales presentation	Product Development/Creative
Sales process	Sales
List of required materials needed from client in order to execute	Product Development
Info on Company A Web site about product	Product Development/Marketing/Creative
Posting of processes and materials on Intranet	Product Development
Education/training of internal staff	Sales/AMs
Schedule/coordinate with outside resources	
Remote people	
Presentation/special internal presenters	
Ongoing training	Product Development
Evaluation of product after 1 month, 3 months and 6 months	Product Development/Sales/Marketing
Internal communication plan	N/A
Announcement at company meeting	Product Development
E-mails	Product Development
Conference calls	

9 Servicing the Customer— The Customer Service Plan

Overview

Customers are the reason your business exists. Good customer service does not just happen, it takes planning, communication and establishing a good rapport with customers to make it happen. Good customer service should be part of your plan.

Customer Service Policy

Define your customer service policy and provide it to customers in writing. Your policy should outline your:

- credit policy
- replacement policy
- return policy
- satisfaction guarantee

Your procedures must be consistent from situation to situation and customer to customer.

> **Hint**
>
> Offering a 100 percent satisfaction or money back guarantee typically increases sales but might also increase the number of customer complaints.

Finding Desirable Customers

Not every customer is a good customer. Only those customers with the ability to pay—and pay on time—for your product or service are desirable customers. Sometimes a customer may have every intention of paying for your product or service, but may not be able to in the end. To keep your financial status healthy, you need to attract and qualify customers who can pay for your product or service. Sometimes you must even fire a customer. Customers who do not pay within a time frame that allows you to make a profit are not good customers. The longer a customer stretches out payments, the less profit you will make. Be selective of your customers. Do not let the promise of big sales distract you from following these basic rules:

Use a Credit Application

If you are extending credit, ask every potential customer to fill out a credit application before you ship the first order or provide initial service. Ask for and check references. A sample credit information request form can be found on the Web landing page www.socrates.com/books/business-plan.aspx.

Ask for a Financial Statement

Before shipping a product or providing service to a first-time customer, ask for a financial statement to review the customer's financial status.

Evaluate Every Applicant

- Does the applicant have the ability to pay?

- Has the applicant agreed to submit payment on time?

- Can you make a reasonable profit on sales on this account?

- If the answer is "only if the applicant pays on time," you have two options: ask for a letter of guarantee from the applicant's bank, or determine if the potential of receiving a late payment is worth the risk.

Check the Applicant's Credit

Check your customers' credit. By extending credit, you are in effect lending money to your customers, and knowing if you are lending money to a good credit risk is good business. It is also wise to request that each customer provide credit references by completing either a "Bank Credit Reference Application" or "New Account Credit Approval Application". These forms can be found on the Web landing page www.socrates.com/books/business-plan.aspx.

Establish terms

Establish credit terms up front. Set up a payment schedule and payment due dates.

Customer Relationship Management (CRM) Program

Prospecting for new customers is expensive—more expensive than retaining your current customers. Creating a CRM program to keep your name in front of customers and to encourage additional sales will not only help you keep your current customers, but it will increase the frequency with which they purchase from your company.

- Create a communication plan to regularly connect with customers.

- Vary your communications to customers.

- Determine what you will communicate to each customer.

Tips for Keeping Customers Satisfied

1. Regularly solicit customer complaints and suggestions by installing a suggestion box.

2. Follow up with new customers by phone to survey their level of satisfaction with your company.

3. Use direct mail surveys to measure overall customer satisfaction. Send surveys to current and past customers.

4. Conduct personal customer interviews to determine overall satisfaction.

5. Hire secret shoppers or customers to determine how customers are being treated by personnel and to see how your employees interact with customers and how well they know your product or service features.

6. Display prominently featured comment cards to encourage customer response.

7. Use toll-free numbers to encourage communications with out-of-town customers and clients.

8. Thoroughly examine every customer complaint for validity and how you can improve your service.

9. Publish a newsletter providing news bulletins, tips and a calendar of events. This will keep your company name in front of the customer.

10. Conduct educational seminars at which you can discuss different features of your business and offer product demonstrations.

11. Reward loyal or frequent customers by offering a discount or special gift to show your appreciation.

12. Train employees on the importance of respecting customers and the value of good customer service.

Set up a Customer Database

Get to know your customers' buying habits and return habits. The best way to do this is to analyze customer purchases. In order to do that, you must first track customer purchases by entering them into a database. Knowing what your customers purchase enables you to effectively cross-promote other products to them. Tracking what customers purchase also allows you to track their returns and reasons for the returns.

Develop a Privacy Policy

Tracking customer purchases and returns is smart customer service, but it may cause customers to be concerned about how you use their data. Will you share the information with other businesses? Will you keep data private—for your company's use only?

Develop a privacy policy and stick to it. Let your customers know if you will be sharing data and provide them with an opt-out option.

Customer Service Professionals

Your customer service professionals are the front line of your business. They may be the first interaction with your company, and therefore they form the customers' first impression. Develop a training program to help them effectively talk with customers—putting your customers first.

Reviewing Returns—Analysis

Review returns monthly. What is the reason for the returns: Product satisfaction? Broken parts? For service products, was the service provided late? Was the service that your company provided substandard or unsatisfactory to the customer?

When analyzing returns, look for patterns. Who are the customers who complain? Do you receive complaints from the same customers on a regular basis?

Keep track of inactive customers and ask them why they no longer purchase your product or service. Conduct mail or phone surveys to past customers or customers who have sent back returns. Analyzing your customers' purchasing and returning habits will help you identify your best customers.

Pulling It All Together

1. Define your customer service policies.

- satisfaction guarantee

- return policy

2. What type of training will you provide customer service representatives?

- dealing with angry customers

- product/service training

- accepting returns

3. Track customer comments. Review customer:

- suggestions

- complaints

- returns—Who is returning products?

4. Qualify your customers.

- Who are your most desirable customers and who are likely to pay?

5. Maintain a customer database.

- Create a checklist of information to track.

- Describe the type of database system you will utilize to store information gathered.

- Develop a privacy policy.

Section Four

10 Smooth Operations— The Operations Plan

Overview

The operations plan summarizes every aspect of operations including procedures, manufacturing equipment, production, facilities and distribution, to name a few. Orchestrating a small business startup involves coordinating a broad range of decisions at once. You must select an affordable yet effective location, obtain ample supplies, equipment and inventory, hire and manage a cohesive staff, and deal with countless legal and financial issues. Such a flood of responsibilities demands a diligent, organized, resourceful person.

Your Operations Plan

- Explain how the business will be managed on a day-to-day basis.
- Explain the structure of your business.
- Discuss hiring and personnel procedures.
- Discuss insurance, lease or rent agreements and related issues pertinent to your business.
- Describe the equipment necessary to produce your products or services.
- Account for production and delivery of products and services.

The Structure of Your Business

Will your business be a sole proprietorship, partnership, S or C corporation, or limited liability company? Short-term considerations include structural regulations, filing fees and record keeping requirements. These are the things that will affect you daily as you run your business.

More importantly, consider long-term factors such as tax benefits, raising capital, transferral of interests and asset protection. Although you may believe you will never fail, the fact is your company has only a 20 percent chance of surviving beyond 5 years. Some entrepreneurs mistakenly feel incorporating is reserved for giant companies employing hundreds and grossing millions. Even single-person companies are eligible for and should consider corporate protection. You can easily obtain the proper forms from your state's Department of Incorporation and fill them out and file them with the secretary of state on your own.

> "Before you incorporate, look at your industry. Do not go immediately to an attorney. You need to become your own expert in your industry. Determine the best legal structure for your business and then consult with the attorney to help ensure your decision is correct and the best for your type of business."
>
> **Sara Shifrin**
> **Director of**
> **Entrepreneur Training**
> **Women's Business**
> **Development Center**
> **Chicago, IL**

Given the proper forms, you can easily form your own corporation, S corporation, limited liability company or limited partnership. Each offers distinct benefits.

Hint
Each state has its own corporation laws. Shop around if location is not an issue for you, but remember that you may have to file as a foreign corporation while operating in a state other than the one in which you are incorporated.

Sole Proprietorships

A sole proprietorship is the least costly way of starting a business. You can form a sole proprietorship by simply opening your doors for business. There are the usual fees for registering your business name and for legal work in changing zoning restrictions and obtaining necessary licenses. Attorney's fees for starting a sole proprietorship will be less than other types of businesses because less document preparation is required.

The advantages include:

- easiest to get started;
- greatest freedom of action;
- maximum authority;
- income tax advantages in very small firms; and
- Social Security advantage to owner.

The disadvantages include:

- unlimited liability;
- death or illness endangers business;
- growth limited to personal energies; and
- personal affairs easily mixed with business.

Sole Proprietorship	
Ownership	Owned and operated by one person
Organizational paperwork	Register your name, get a business license and start operating
Personal liability	Owners have unlimited liability—personal assets are at risk in event of failure or lawsuit
Tax forms (minimum)	Filed with personal income tax return—Form 1040, Schedule C, Schedule SE (Self-Employment Tax), Form 4562

Upside: You have sole responsibility for the business.
Downside: You have sole responsibility for the business.

Partnerships

A partnership can be formed by simply making an oral agreement between two or more persons, but such informality is not recommended. Legal fees for drawing up a partnership agreement are higher than those for a sole proprietorship but may be lower than for incorporating. You would be wise, however, to consult an attorney to have a partnership agreement drawn up to help avoid future disputes.

When choosing a partner, ask yourself these questions:

• **What does the enterprise need?**
• **What is someone good at; what are they better at than someone else?**
• **What do they like to do?**

If you can get the answers to those questions to triangulate, that is pretty good. Usually, it does not work that way; usually, it has more to do with what somebody is not good at or what they do not like to do. Responsibilities get carved around that more than anything else. The first priority should be that all aspiring entrepreneurs should look at themselves in the mirror regularly to try to identify what are their failings, what are their weaknesses, where do they need to be supported the most? Most small businesses do not become much bigger businesses because of the inherent failing of the entrepreneur. Sometimes it's market conditions or the capitalization of the company. But the majority of the time it's the limitations of that individual.

It goes back to Socrates…know thyself.

William Lederer
Chairman & CEO
Minotaur Capital Management
Chicago, IL

The advantages of partnership include:

- two heads are better than one;
- additional resources of venture capital; and
- better credit rating than corporation of similar size.

The disadvantages of partnership include:

- death, withdrawal or bankruptcy of one partner endangers the business;
- difficult to get rid of a bad partner; and
- hazy line of authority.

General Partnershp	
Ownership	Owned and operated by two or more people
Your level of control	Evenly split among partners
Organizational paperwork	Easy to organize, but you need legal contracts drawn up for the partners
Personal liability	Owners have unlimited liability—personal assets are at risk in event of failure or lawsuit
Tax forms (minimum)	In addition to personal income tax forms (1040, Schedule SE, Form 4562), you must file a Form 1065 (Partnership Return of Income)

Upside: Both parties share in the investment and operation.
Downside: Partners could end up disagreeing, creating legal problems. Each partner is accountable for the other partners' actions.

Limited Partnership	
Ownership	Owned and operated by two or more people
Your level of control	Amount of investment and responsibilities of the individual partners are determined by contractual delineation
Organizational paperwork	Register your name, get a business license and start operating
Personal liability	Owners have unlimited liability unless stipulated by contracts between partners
Tax forms (minimum)	In addition to personal income tax forms (1040, Schedule SE, Form 4562), you must file a Form 1065 (Partnership Return of Income)

Upside: Other parties share in the investment and operation.
Downside: Partners could end up disagreeing, creating legal problems.

Partnerships may take on additional forms:

Secret Partnership

The partners are active in the ventures but are unknown to the public.

Silent Partners

Partners are usually inactive and have only a financial interest in the partnership.

Limited Partnership Agreement

Drawing up a partnership agreement is very important when forming a partnership. Whether you are forming a partnership with family members, best friends or business acquaintances, it is important to define the partnership on paper.

A legally binding partnership agreement should include the following:

1. The legal name of the partnership.

2. The nature of your business.

3. The type of partnership–limited, general, secret, silent.

4. How long the partnership is to last–as with most contracts it needs a start and end date.

5. What each of the partners will contribute to the partnership–capital, in-kind goods, services, etc. This is referred to as initial capitalization.

6. Any sales, loans or leases to the partnership by the partners listed in detail.

7. The management structure of the partnership–who will be responsible for what areas or tasks?

8. The sales of a partnership interest–a clause may be added that restricts a partner's right to sell his or her interest to third parties. It should provide, however, a method of allowing the partner to divest his or her interest in the partnership without bringing in outsiders.

9. A clause that will allow the partnership to be dissolved.

10. A survival clause in the event one partner leaves or dies.

11. Guidelines for how disputes will be resolved–either through mediation, legal, etc.

Hint

If a partnership agreement is not executed, then all partners are equal under the law.

Corporations

A corporation is formed and authorized by law to act as a single entity, although it may be owned by one or more persons. It is legally endowed with rights and responsibilities and has a life of its own, independent of the owners and operators. It has been defined by the U.S. Supreme Court as "an artificial being, invisible and existing only in contemplation of the law." Think of it as a distinct and independent entity that exists separately from its owners.

Limited Liability

The owners are not personally liable for debts and obligations of the corporation. They can personally lose only to the extent of their investment in the corporation, with the exception that they may be personally liable for certain types of taxes, such as payroll taxes withheld from the employees' paychecks but not paid to the Internal Revenue Service and state tax authorities. If the business fails or loses a lawsuit, the general creditors cannot attach the owners' homes, cars and other personal property.

Transferable Interests

A corporation has the ability to raise capital by issuing shares of stock, whether public or private. Although the sale of public stock is highly regulated by both federal and state governments, ownership interest or shares of stock may be freely transferred to another party under the rules of the stockholder agreement. Once the interest is transferred, the new owner has all the rights and privileges associated with the former owner's interest. The Federal Trade Commission sets strict rules for issuing and publicly trading shares.

Tax Deductions

The IRS allows corporate owners to fully deduct certain fringe benefits, such as pensions, retirement plans and other profit-sharing plans, if properly documented.

Continuous Life

Unlike a partnership or sole proprietorship, a corporation has a life independent of its owners and may continue to exist despite the death and incapacity of any or all of its directors.

Remember to Register

In order to gain access to free forms, dictionaries, checklists and updates, readers must register their book purchase at Socrates.com. An eight-digit Registration Code is provided on the enclosed CD. See page iv for further details.

Forming a corporation involves five major drawbacks:

1. Double taxation–A corporation generates its own profit and is thus taxed separately from its members. Owners are also taxed on an individual basis, meaning a corporation is subject to double taxation (which may be avoided with a Subchapter S corporation only if dividends are distributed).

2. Bureaucracy and governmental regulation–In order for the IRS to recognize a corporation as a separate entity, its directors must abide by strict regulations that govern corporate activity. Without well-maintained corporate records, the courts may disregard your corporate status and allow creditors to sue you personally for business debts. This is called piercing the corporate veil, and happens more often than you think. States require you to file your articles of incorporation and sometimes bylaws, but to safely protect your corporate status, you must dutifully record all your meetings, resolutions and amendments, and file corporate reports. You must also inform the secretary of state of any other changes involving your directors, registered agents, location or corporate purpose.

3. Costs–Corporations are the most expensive form of business to organize.

4. Operating across state lines–This can be complicated. Corporations need to qualify to do business in states where they are not incorporated.

5. Ending the corporate existence–Ending, and in many cases even changing, the structure of the organization, can be more complicated and costly than for other business entities.

Corporation	
Ownership	Owned by shareholders
Your level of control	Checked by your board of directors
Organizational paperwork	Must file articles of corporation and is continually monitored by local, state and federal agencies
Personal liability	Shareholders have limited liability of the corporation's debts
Tax forms (minimum)	Form 1120 (Corporation Income Tax Return), Form 8109-B (Deposit Coupon), Form 4265 (Depreciation)

Upside: You can raise money by issuing stock.
Downside: Taxes will be higher overall because dividends to shareholders are not deductible from business income.

S Corporation

Once you have incorporated, you may have the option of filing taxes under IRS Subchapter S. An S corporation has the corporate structure of a C or regular corporation but enjoys the same pass-through tax status as a partnership, sole proprietorship or limited liability company. This means the S corporation itself avoids double taxation, paying no federal taxes. There are a few things to remember. Your salary must be included on the payroll and is subject to employment taxes. Health benefits are not fully deductible as in a C corporation. However, an S corporation is allowed to carry back losses from prior years to offset current earnings.

S Corporation	
Ownership	Owned by shareholders
Your level of control	Checked by your board of directors
Organizational paperwork	Must file articles of incorporation and is continually monitored by local, state and federal agencies
Personal liability	Shareholders have limited liability of the corporation's debts
Tax forms (minimum)	Form 1120 (Corporation Income Tax Return), Form 8109-B (Deposit Coupon), Form 4265 (Depreciation)

Upside: You can raise money by issuing stock and treat earnings as distributions passing directly through to shareholders and their personal tax returns.
Downside: Any shareholders working for the company must pay themselves wages, meeting the standards of reasonable compensation.

CLimited Liability Companies

To some business analysts, the limited liability company (LLC) represents the best of both worlds. First, it offers the pass-through tax status of a partnership. Members are taxed on an individual basis. The company itself pays no taxes, unlike a C corporation. Second, members also enjoy limited liability protection. Risk is limited to their business investment. Personal assets are not subject to seizure from the company's creditors. Both advantages come with relatively few structural and paperwork requirements.

Most states require LLCs to register their articles of organization (similar to corporate articles of incorporation), the operating agreement (similar to corporate bylaws or a partnership agreement) and pay a fee. Check with your secretary of state for statutes that may apply to you. See Chapter 20: Planning Worksheets for an "LLC Company Operating Agreement."

The disadvantages of operating as an LLC include the lack of widespread familiarity and thus acceptance of this type of organization. IRS rules governing insolvency may create problems for the owners of an LLC. LLCs do not enjoy the advantages of IRS rulings when there is a sale of worthless stock or stock is sold at a loss. The sale of 50 percent or more of the ownership of the LLC in any 12-month period ends any tax advantage the company may have had with the IRS, and LLCs may not engage in tax-free reorganizations.

Limited Liability Company (LLC)	
Ownership	Owned and operated by members or can be structured as manager managed
Your level of control	Total
Organizational paperwork	For most states, must file articles of corporation
Personal liability	Limited liability—owner's personal assets are not at risk
Tax forms (minimum)	Depending on the structure, taxed as a partnership or corporation
Upside: You have the control of a sole proprietorship with the protection of a corporation. **Downside:** You have to deal with the paperwork of a corporation.	

TINs and EINs

Employer Identification Numbers (EINs)

An EIN, also known as a federal Tax Identification Number (TIN), is a nine-digit number (for example, 12-3456789) assigned to sole proprietors, corporations, partnerships, estates, trusts and other entities for tax filing and reporting purposes. It is used to identify a business entity.

You can apply for an EIN online at www.irs.gov by completing Form SS-4. The information you provide on this form will establish your business tax account. Print the instructions for easy reference prior to completing your online Form SS-4 application. The form is also available online at local IRS offices and at all Social Security offices.

If you would rather apply by phone, contact the IRS Business and Specialty Tax Line.

Hint
An EIN is for use in connection with your business activities only. Do NOT use your EIN in place of your Social Security number.

Who Must File an SS-4

You must file this form if you have not been assigned an EIN before and:

- you pay wages to one or more employees, including household employees;

- you are required to have an EIN to use on any return, statement or other document, even if you are not an employer;

- you are a withholding agent required to withhold taxes on income, other than wages, paid to a nonresident alien (individual, corporation, partnership, etc.). A withholding agent may be an agent, broker, fiduciary, manager, tenant or spouse and is required to file Form 1042, Annual Withholding Tax Return for U.S. Source Income of Foreign Persons; or

- you file Schedule C, Profit or Loss From Business, Schedule C-EZ, Net Profit From Business, or Schedule F, Profit or Loss From Farming, or Form 1040, U.S. Individual Income Tax Return, and have a Keogh plan or are required to file excise, employment, or alcohol, tobacco or firearms returns.

How to Apply

Online

Not all businesses may use this method. An EIN will be issued after the successful submission of the completed Form SS-4 online. For more information or to see if your business can apply online, visit www.irs.gov/businesses/small.

Mail or Telephone

Complete Form SS-4 to apply for an EIN either by mail or telephone. You can get an EIN within minutes by calling IRS Tele-TIN or sending the completed Form SS-4 to your local IRS Service Center to receive your EIN by mail.

You should apply for your EIN early so that you have it when you need to file a tax return or make a deposit. You can get an EIN quickly by calling the Tele-TIN phone number for your state. If you prefer, you can fax a completed Form SS-4 to the IRS Service Center, and they will respond with a return fax in about 1 week. If you apply by mail, send your completed Form SS-4 at least 4 to 5 weeks before you need your EIN to file a return or make a deposit.

> **Note**
>
> If you do not have your EIN by the time a tax return is due, write "applied for" and the date you applied in the space shown for the number. Do not use your Social Security number.

If you do not have your EIN by the time a tax deposit is due, send your payment to the Service Center address for your state. Make your check or money order payable to Internal Revenue Service and include your name as shown on the SS-4, address, tax type, period covered and the date you applied for your EIN. Your taxpayer identification number may be your Social Security number or state issued EIN. These numbers are required by the IRS and companies as a method of tracking your earnings and will appear on your 1099s.

In order to open a business account at a local bank, you will need either an EIN or state confirmation of a Doing Business As (DBA) filing with the state.

DBA

A fictitious business name, assumed name or DBA allows you to legally do business as a particular name at minimal cost and without having to create an entirely new business entity. You can accept payments, advertise and otherwise present yourself under that name. In fact, if you present your business under a name other than your proper legal name without proper notification, it may be considered fraud. Fortunately, filing for an assumed name is easy and inexpensive.

Filing an assumed name allows you as a sole proprietor to use a business name rather than your personal name. In most states, you cannot open a business bank account or accept payments without a registered DBA.

The exact rules vary from country to country and from state to state within the United States, so check with your local business regulatory authority regarding your area. But if there is any implication that there are more people involved (Sanford & Sons, The Mehle Group), or if you just use the first name (Sam's Hardware Store, Fred's Boathouse), you have to file an assumed name. It also lets you use a typical business name without creating a formal legal entity— corporation, partnership, LLC. You can even open a business checking account and get a business phone listing for the name. For sole proprietors, this is the least expensive way to legally do business under a business name.

A DBA allows a single legal entity–corporation, LLC, etc–to operate multiple businesses without creating a new legal entity for each business. For example, if you are planning to operate a series of Web sites or a chain of stores, you might set up a corporation with a generic name–such as ABC Web Enterprises, Inc., or The Retailer, LLC–and then file an assumed name for each Web site or store. Since there is significant expense in filing and maintaining a corporation, this helps control costs while still allowing you to expand your business.

Applying for an Assumed Name

In some U.S. states, you register your assumed name with an individual state's secretary of state or other state agency, but in most states, registration is handled at the county level, and each county may have different forms and fees for registering a name. The process is simple: You perform a search through the state or county database to make sure the name is not already in use, then submit a simple form along with the correct filing fee—anywhere from $10 to $50. Some states also require that you publish a notice in your local newspaper and submit an affidavit to show that you have fulfilled the publication requirement. Call your county clerk's office to find out the local fees and procedures in your area.

Location

Your choice of location may be tied directly to your target market, or it may be an accessibility choice—close to a major highway or adjacent to rail lines, for example. Include a description of your location as follows:

XYZ Company, LLC has leased 1,000 square feet of office space located at 1234 First Ave, Chicago, IL. This space was chosen for the building's close proximity to public transportation, excellent security system, low square footage costs, flexible leasing arrangements and the option to lease additional space when needed.

The office features three individual offices of 10 feet by 10 feet in size; a common area for desks that is 10 feet by 30 feet, and a 20-foot by 20-foot conference room with a small reception area. The office will comfortably hold up to six individuals. Careful consideration was made prior to selecting the site. Our site selection worksheet outlining our requirements and parameters is attached, as is a copy of our lease agreement.

We viewed a number of additional sites before selecting 1234 First Ave. Other available sites were not selected for the following reasons: a limited number of parking facilities nearby and the risk of higher parking rates;offices that were not easily accessible by public transportation; higher crime rate for other neighborhoods than average; or the building's amenities were inadequate— electrical was not updated or the building was not wired for Internet access.

Complete a worksheet for each location visited. Observe and record your observations and then compare the features of each site with your requirements.

Site Selection Worksheet

Physical Address:_____

_____

Name, address, phone number of realtor or leasing agent:_____

_____

Square footage cost: _____

History of location: _____

_____

Location of space in relation to your target market: _____

_____

Traffic patterns for customers: _____

Traffic patterns for suppliers: _____

Loading and unloading accessibility: _____

Loading and unloading restrictions: _____

Availability of parking (include diagram):_____

Accessibility to public transportation: _____

Crime statistics for the area:_____

Location of public sercies (police, fire): _____

_____

List type of neighboring shops and local businesses (number of retail shops, office buildings, restaurants, etc.):_____

_____

Zoning regulations: _____

Adequacy of utilities: _____

Availability of raw materials/supplies: _____

Availability of labor force:_____

Labor rate of pay for the area: _____

Housing available for employees: _____

Tax rates (state, county, income, payroll, city tax, special assesment):_____

_____

Evaluation of site in relation to competition: _____

_____

Notes on walking tour of the area: _____

_____

Management and Personnel

An important part of your daily operations is positioning of management and employees. Include a description of:

Labor Force

What is your available labor force? Do you have a good supply of workers, or will you need to recruit qualified individuals from outside the area?

Management

How many managers will be needed to oversee important areas? Provide an organizational flow chart showing responsibilities and oversights. Include how many people each manager will supervise.

Employees and Personnel

How many employees will you need to hire to operate the company efficiently? Provide a timeline or milestones as guidelines to hiring additional staff.

Key people

Provide a short description of each of your key people including their education and past experiences and what experience they will bring to the company.

Personnel Plan

How quickly do you anticipate bringing on additional help? Will they be part-time or full-time?

Subcontracting/Outsourcing

Can some positions be outsourced—which ones and at what cost?

Compensation

Describe how each employee will be compensated: salaries, benefits, bonuses, vacation time or stock purchase plans.

Recruiting

How will you hire employees? In this section, provide a list of current employees and expected payroll for the year and then follow up with a hiring plan for the year. Break out payroll expenses by month and compare with your projected revenues and expenses by month to determine staffing projections. If your sales are seasonal, with the majority of your revenues earned in the last quarter of the year, seasonal or temporary help might make the most economical sense.

Supply and Distribution Strategy

Provide a description of your ordering or production process. If you are distributing products, what is the process for ordering product? If you are a manufacturer, what is the timeline for production?

- What is your main means of distribution?
- What is the timeline of ordering supplies?

Suppliers

How you selected your suppliers is important to investors. How do you choose your suppliers and vendors? Are there alternative vendors available? Do you receive favorable rates from one vendor versus another? What is the difference in quality?

Production

What is the process for production? Do you have a timeline?

Pricing

Describe your pricing policies. What is the average selling price per product— wholesale, direct to the customer or retail?

Unit Sales per Product/Service

What is the average unit sale of each product or service?

Average Sales Price

Does the customer purchase multiple units with each sale?

Average Days to Ship

What is the average number of days from order date to shipping date?

Inventory

Maintaining controls on the amount of inventory or how often inventory is ordered can make a difference in your profit level. What inventory controls do you have in place? How often do you take inventory?

Efficiency Control

Are there processes in place to track order progress and to determine if orders are being handled efficiently?

Fulfillment

Where does product fulfillment take place—on premises or off?

Insurance

Insurance is an important consideration for every business. Protecting your business from common claims and serious disruptions and risks will keep your business operational. There are a number of different types of insurance you can procure depending on your business type.

Product liability is especially important in certain industries. Service businesses are concerned about personal liability and insuring empoyees during transportation. If a vehicle is used for business purposes, the vehicle must be insured. If you own a building, your building must also be covered by hazard and liability insurance. Some types of businesses require bonding insurance. Partners may want life insurance on each other with the other partner as the beneficiary. Medical, disability and life insurance may be offered to employees as well.

Umbrella Insurance

Your primary business insurance typically protects you against the usual kinds of loss–fire, theft, etc–but you would be responsible for any amount beyond your policy limits. A commercial umbrella insurance policy provides liability protection up to a limit you select over and above the limits of your primary policy.

The policy provides coverage over your primary policies in these key areas:

- general liability
- garage liability
- auto liability
- employer's liability

You can choose your own level of coverage, anywhere from $1 million to $5 million or more. Your premium cost depends on the nature and location of your business, the liability limit you choose and the number of buildings and vehicles you want covered.

Life Insurance for Businesses

Life insurance is an important consideration for business owners. It can keep a business operating by providing ready funds in the form of a death benefit should something happen to a business owner or a key employee. If you are self-employed, your business is an important part of your life and surely depends on you for its successful operation. Whether your company is a sole proprietorship, a partnership or a corporation, you need to anticipate the day when the death of the owner or a key employee may dramatically affect and jeopardize its future.

Key Person Life Insurance

Key person life insurance is insurance to protect your business against financial loss due to the death of a key employee. If one of your top employees dies and you have key person life insurance insuring that person, the business will receive a life insurance death benefit payment that can help offset potential losses and provide money to attract and train a replacement.

Maintaining an Insurance Log

If you maintain a variety of policies with different insurance carriers, keeping each policy straight can be a daunting task. Make it easy on yourself and create a company insurance log. In your log you should record the insurance company's name, the agent's name, phone number and e-mail information, the type of insurance policy you have with the company, the coverage, period covered, costs and any other notes of interest. Maintaining an insurance log will make it easier to plan your annual budget, and if you need to make a claim, all the information will be right at your fingertips.

Record each type of insurance policy you may have as shown on the next page.

Company Insurance Log

Your company name here:

Insurance company	Contact person	Type of insurance and policy number	Description of coverage	Cost/year	Coverage period	Notes
American Family	Fred Smith 555-222-5151	Building and product liability Policy # 56930-9032234	Replacement policy on building and $5 million product liability coverage	$700	Jan. 1 through Dec. 31	Order a new appraisal on building
Aetna Health	Suzie Jones 555-333-5555	Employee health Policy # 5632211	Health, dental, life	$4,000 per employee	Jan. 1 through Dec. 31	New policy
State Farm	Joan Pierce 555-444-7777	Auto Policy # 89654325566	Coverage for sales cars	$2,000/car	Mar. 1 through Mar. 28	Review policy at end of term

This log is also available in Chapter 20: Planning Worksheets.

Buy-Sell Agreements

Contact your insurance agent to discuss the advantages of funding a buy-sell agreement with life insurance.

Hint
Buy-sell agreements must be prepared by a qualified attorney who is familiar with your business and personal circumstances. Tax implications should be discussed with a qualified tax consultant.

Security

As many as one-third of all businesses fail as a result of poor security. Security does not always involve theft of equipment or supplies; it can also be theft of information. The theft of information may be the leaking of information about future strategic plans or new product concepts. It may also include the theft of client information from outside hackers who may have gained entry into your system or from renegade or disgruntled employees.

In an age where conducting business electronically is commonplace, it is a must to create an electronic security system to protect customer information from hackers or intruders in your system. Equally as important, you also need to protect your own proprietary information.

Policies and Procedures

In order to run efficiently, every operation must have policies and procedures in place. Outline your purchasing policies and procedures. To keep controls on spending, you may institute a monthly spending cap or grant only one or two employees spending power. Other checks may include requiring more than one person to sign off on all purchase orders or credit card purchases. What controls do you have in place to deter excessive spending?

Capital Expenditures

A capital expenditure is a purchase of an item that will last more than 12 months. Describe your current equipment and a list of equipment you plan to purchase during the next 12 to 24 months. Explain why each capital expenditure is necessary and what benefit each will produce for your company. Provide detail on expenditures by month to create a capital spending budget.

Technology Plans

Technology is constantly changing and improving. New technology is bound to have an impact on your business. Describe any technology plans scheduled to be implemented within the next 12 to 24 months. Provide a thorough, detailed description of the benefits of the new technology, how it will affect your current business and how much the plan will cost. Break the plan into smaller segments and costs.

Pulling It All Together

Answer the following questions to create a complete operations plan:

Describe how the business will be managed on a day-to-day basis.

Outline the management structure of your business. Provide a flowchart diagram.

Discuss your hiring and personnel plan for the year.

Include all information about insurance, lease or rent agreements, and related issues pertinent to your business. List all insurance policies including key person life insurance policies for partners or key personnel.

List all equipment necessary to produce your products or services.

Describe production and delivery of products and services.

Describe the legal structure of your business.

Explain why you selected your location. Include a copy of your lease agreement.

Provide a list of current employees and expected payroll for the year.

Break out payroll expenses by month and compare it to your projected revenues and expenses by month to determine staffing projections.

Provide a description of your ordering or production process.

If you are distributing products, what is the process for ordering product? If you are a manufacturer, what is the timeline for production?

Describe your main means of distribution.

What is the timeline for ordering supplies?

Summarize how you chose your suppliers and vendors.

Are there alternative vendors available?

Do you receive favorable rates from one vendor versus another?

What is the difference in quality?

What is the process for production? Do you have a timeline?

Describe your pricing policies. What is the average selling price per product—wholesale, direct to the customer or retail?

What is the average unit sale of each product?

What is your average sales price? Does the customer purchase multiple units with each sale?

What is the average number of days from order to shipping date?

Describe any inventory controls you have in place.

Where does product fulfillment take place—on premises or off?

11 Building the Team

Overview

Behind every successful entrepreneur is a solid management team. One of the most important elements of your business plan is the section that provides information about why you and your management team are the most qualified individuals to start and run this new venture. Knowing that you want your business to grow, you will also want to describe your organizational structure, incentives you may offer to attract qualified personnel and a description of the jobs they will be holding.

Organizational Structure

Draw an organizational chart showing the assignment of responsibilities of each major business activity.

What does it look like? Who owns what and who reports to whom?

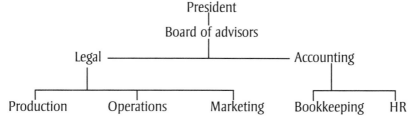

There Are Different Types of Organizations

Basic Design

Put somebody on top and let everyone else do all the jobs that have to be done. Everyone is equal. This is considered a flat organizational chart with one manager leading multiple departments and many employees.

Advantages

You can always find someone to do whatever is needed to get the job done.

Disadvantages

This design works well with companies of fewer than 20 employees. It is more difficult with more than 20 people because the person at the top will begin to have difficulty keeping track of everyone.

Functional Model

Organize your business around business functions. Divide people into groups depending on their skill levels or what they have an interest in. Each group will have a manager to oversee the group. This model segments workers into clearly defined groups such as marketing, operations, accounting, production and customer service.

Advantages

This format works well if your business has only one type of product or service. Employees can focus on one job and can become really good at it. Everyone knows exactly what they are responsible for because jobs are clearly defined. It provides an excellent way to measure how everyone is doing.

Disadvantages

Eventually, each group may become isolated and may not share information well with the other teams. Each group may begin to have separate goals not necessarily tied to the corporate mission. Communication may break down, leaving a company that does not have a singular vision.

Divisional Form

If a company is large enough to be involved in more than one business, adopt a divisional organization. Each division is responsible for a particular product, service, market or geographic area.

Advantages

Organizations divided into divisions encourage each group to focus its energy into the part of the business it is in. Each division can concentrate on its own set of customers, competitors and company issues.

Disadvantages

Separate divisions may have some overlap in product and marketing strategies resulting in competition for the same customer. A divisional organization may mean greater overhead costs because each division has its own management layers, operations, research, marketing, sales and finance areas.

Matrix Format

This format organizes people along two dimensions. Employees engage in multitasking and may report to two different managers.

Advantages

This format allows you to share talents, expertise and experience throughout your company as needed.

Disadvantages

It may cause tension and confusion because employees are reporting to two bosses who may have different priority levels that may not be effectively communicated or shared between areas.

Flexibility is key—your organizational structure must change as your company's direction changes.

Management Philosophy

What is your management style? Are you a risk taker? Are you a hands-off manager who expects employees to make decisions?

> "If there is a preferred skill set for the CEO of any business, on average, you would really like that person to be a moneymaker. A close second is a great salesperson, a great advocate on behalf of her company, products and services to others who can influence the ability to create revenue for the enterprise."
>
> **William Lederer**
> **Chairman & CEO**
> **Minotaur Capital Management**
> **Chicago, IL**

Key Personnel Incentives

What types of incentives will you offer key management to keep them with the company?

Key Personnel Responsibilities and Duties

Define your management team. List the key individuals who will make up your core management team. Indicate additional staff you will add as needed.

Draft Your Business Accomplishment Resume of Yourself and Key Management

Prepare a personal history of principals. Include five key elements:

- personal work history
- related work experience
- duties and responsibilities of key personnel
- salaries
- resources available to the business

History of Principals

What makes you and your partners qualified to run this business successfully? Spell out your past experiences, how they relate to this new venture and how you will make this business successful. Include the following information:

- State your business background.
- Include all management experience you have had.
- Provide all formal and informal education experience that is relevant to your management abilities.
- Include your age, special abilities and reasons for going into business, past companies you have worked for, where you have lived.
- Describe your physical condition. Do you have the stamina needed to perform the job?

- Why do you think you will be successful in this job?

- What is your personal financial status? Draft your personal financial statement. List all personal collateral. Include assets and liabilities—stocks, insurance policies, automobiles, bank statements, etc.

Related Work Experience

- Provide an overview of how your work experience will benefit the company.

- Provide a description of any direct operational experience you may have within the industry.

- List any managerial experience you may have in this industry.

- Explain any other managerial experience you may have outside this industry.

- Keep in mind that relevant experience is a plus and reduces transition time and possible conflicts among management.

Duties and Responsibilities

Define the roles of each manager in advance. Carefully define:

- who does what;

- who reports to whom;

- who owns what; and

- who makes the final decisions.

Allocating duties and responsibilities is a very important step in keeping operations running smoothly. Make sure your managers know what they are responsible for and that they have the absolute authority to make decisions.

Salaries

Keep salary expectations realistic. Determine your salary budgets and then add 15 percent for contingencies. To help you determine your salary requirements, complete the following "Salary Guideline Worksheet."

Based on an average month, how much do you need to cover basic living expenses?

Monthly Salary Guideline Worksheet

Fixed Monthly Payments	
House or rent payment—interest, principle, insurance, taxes	$
Car payments, including insurance	$
Credit card payments	$
Home improvement loan payments	$
Personal loan payments	$
Health plan payments	$
Life insurance premiums	$
Other insurance premiums	$
Savings/investments	$
Miscellaneous payments	$
Total	$

Household Operating Expenses	
Telephone	$
Gas and electricity	$
Water	$
Cable	$
Other household expenses, repairs, maintenance	$
Assessments	$
Total	$

Personal Expenses	
Clothing, cleaning, laundry	$
Prescription medications	$
Physicians, dentists	$
Education	$
Clubs/Dues	$
Gifts and contributions	$
Travel	$
Newspapers, magazines, books	$
Auto upkeep and gas	$
Spending money and allowances	$
Miscellaneous	$
Total	$

Food	
Food at home	$
Food away from home	$
Total	$

Other Expenses	$
Federal and state taxes	$
Miscellaneous taxes	$
Total	$

Budget Summary	
Gross income—monthly total	$
Less Expenses:	$
Fixed monthly payments	$
Household operating expenses	$
Personal expenses	$
Food expenses	$
Tax expenses	$
Monthly Total	$
Monthly Total Expenses	$

Give Yourself a Title

Even if your business is a one-person venture, give yourself a title. Every business needs structure.

Building a Board of Advisors

> "The trick to managing any investor is to only give an investor as much power and authority as you are comfortable with. All that money comes with a price."
>
> **Kelly Mizeur**
> **Finance Counselor**
> **Women's Business Development Center**
> **Chicago, IL**

A board of advisors serves a different function than a board of directors. A board of advisors provides essential guidance, information and services to your new venture. Often the board will play devil's advocate, pointing out potential flaws in what you are doing. It is a tremendous think tank resource to keep you on track and find the resources you need to succeed.

Advisors usually serve unpaid and do not have voting power when it comes to major company decisions and the hiring and firing of executives and officers. They are usually reimbursed for travel expenses in recognition of their dedication of time and service. Most advisors anticipate and expect additional phone calls seeking advice between scheduled meetings. Advisory committees usually meet two to four times a year to review finances, ideas, proposed product developments, and sales and marketing strategies.

Advisory members are generally professionals with the expertise and contacts you need to fill a gap in your own management team. Your advisors will have a strong belief in what you are doing and want to be a part of your new business.

There is a distinct difference between a board of advisors and a board of directors. A board of directors has a greater level of influence over the management team and is capable of taking control from the founders if the board disagrees with the plans that the team is making and the direction in which the team is headed.

Forming an Advisory Board

Building an advisory board with a variety of talents will provide you with varied opinions about your business. For example, to blend together the best talents for your business, invite a banker, lawyer, industry expert, accountant, chief financial officer, business consultant, one or two successful business owners and a technology expert to join your advisory board. The diverse professional skills of your board will help you view your business from many different angles.

The length of time an advisor serves may be as short as 1 year or as long as 5 years. Some companies design their terms to be 1 year with renewal options so if an advisor becomes too busy to serve, he or she may be replaced with minimal disruption.

To form an advisory board:

1. Identify the kinds of people you need on your board.

2. Interview candidates by phone. Present to the candidate what you are looking for.

3. Follow up the phone interview with a letter. Provide the candidate with an overview of the board, the responsibilities and your expectations.

4. Follow up the letter with a telephone invitation to the prospective board member to visit your company along with other board members.

During the tour, ask questions about why the candidates are interested in serving on your board, whether they have served on any other boards and what they have accomplished for those companies, and how they think they will contribute to your company.

The ideal candidate will ask you many questions about your company and will be genuinely interested in helping your company grow.

Pulling It All Together

1. Identifying key team members in your business plan shows investors a lot about your team structure.

2. Draw an organizational chart showing the assignment of responsibilities of each major business activity. What does it look like? Who owns what and who reports to whom?

3. Describe how your business is organized:

• basic design	• functional model
• divisional format	• matrix format

4. What is your management style? How will you lead your employees?

5. What types of incentives will you offer key management to keep them with the company?

6. Define your management team.

7. List the key individuals who will make up your core management team. Indicate additional staff you will add as needed.

8. Include a management resume for each key team member in your business plan document. Include the following five key elements:

- personal work history
- related work experience
- salary history
- resources available to the business
- duties and responsibilities of key personnel

9. Define the roles of each manager in advance. Carefully define:

- who does what
- who reports to whom
- who owns what
- who makes final decisions

10. Based on an average month, determine how much you will need to cover basic living expenses.

11. Give yourself a title.

12. Form an advisory board.

Learning the Language of Business

Readers are entitled to full access and use of the comprehensive Business Law and Accounting & Finance Dictionaries found on the Web landing page at www.socrates.com/books/business-plan. aspx. Please remember to register the first time you use this free resource. See page iv for instructions.

12 Financially Speaking— The Financial Plan

Overview

Most businesses fail simply because they were undercapitalized. Estimating and planning your business capital requirements is one of the most important steps in starting a successful business. A successful idea must be backed up by a credible financial plan. The financial part of the business plan is designed to attract potential lenders and investors to your business. The smart lender or investor wants to be sure that the financial projections of the business are realistic.

The financial plan is often neglected by entrepreneurs who do not like to work with numbers or simply may not understand them. Before you launch your business, you first should do your research to develop financial goals and assign key milestone dates that will help you measure whether your business is meeting your goals.

Working Capital

Working Capital is defined as the excess of current assets over current liabilities.

Current assets are the most liquid and most easily convertible to cash. Current liabilities are obligations due within 1 year. Therefore, working capital measures what is available to pay a company's current debt. It also represents the cushion or margin of protection a company can give its short-term creditors.

Working capital is essential for a company to meet its continuous operational needs. Its adequacy influences a firm's ability to meet its trade and short-term debt obligations, as well as to remain financially viable.

> **Hint**
>
> The number one cause of business failure is a lack of cash flow or money to keep producing while awaiting receipts. Always make certain you have money or a credit line earmarked for meeting short-term expenses during business lulls.

Capital Requirements

How much do you need to start your business? The money you need to start or expand your business can be divided into two categories:

Capital Investment

This is how much cash you will need to spend before you can open your business.

Initial Working Capital

This is the amount of cash reserves you need to keep your business afloat before you begin to show a profit every month.

If your initial cash flow forecasts show a negative cash flow the first few months of operation you will need to have a little extra cash set aside. Your initial working capital keeps the doors open until the cash flow from monthly business becomes positive.

> **"Ideally, it would be nice to have a year's reserve on hand. But realistically, investors may be hard pressed to loan or have the business tie up that much money for that length of time. I encourage people to do cash flow projections plan to determine how much additional capital is needed to keep the business from running out of money, plus having another 3-month reserve so you can make the mistakes that you probably will make."**
>
> **Sara Shifrin**
> **Director of**
> **Entrepreneur Training**
> **Women's Business**
> **Development Center**
> **Chicago, IL**

Prepare Your Capital Spending Plan

Your capital spending plan includes all of the things you have to buy in order to open for business. The list of items may include:

- initial inventory
- furniture
- fixtures
- equipment
- computer equipment and telephones
- business license
- deposits for lease
- insurance

To understand how much capital you will need to start your business, create a capital equipment list. Start by writing down every item you think you will need to have in place before starting your business. Next, estimate the cost of each item, and you will have a good idea of your capital requirements.

A checklist of common items businesses need to open for business can be divided into two groups—Capital Items and Expense Items.

Hint

Capital items are generally viewed as permanent items—such as equipment and furniture—that are one-time purchases, have a useful life of more than 1 year and may be expensed or depreciated for tax purposes.

Expense items are shown as either fixed expenses or as a cost of sale at their time of purchase. They generally last less than 1 year and may be expensed for tax purposes but not depreciated.

Suggestions for keeping expenses low:

- Keep an eye on your expenses.
- Do not go out there living like you are still a corporate person, still getting a big salary.
- There are ways now that you can use a downtown address with a business suite with an answering service to make people think you have a downtown office and a downtown mailing address while operating out of the suburbs.
- In retail, the biggest downfall is leasehold improvements—to build out a restaurant, yoga center or spa is a big expense.
- Hire as you go. That is true with most expenses; expand once you can afford it.
- If you promote, make sure you can deliver the goods if business picks up.
- Hire staff on a freelance or per-project basis. This will free up payroll expenses for promotion or development.
- Watch your overhead—regardless of the business. Make sure that you are spending your money on what is going to [grow] your business.

Kelly Mizeur
Finance Counselor
Women's Business Development Center
Chicago, IL

A Typical Capital Items Checklist

__ Permanent signs, heaters, air conditioners, cooking and refrigeration equipment

__ Automobiles for sales, trucks for deliveries, vans for equipment

__ Equipment, including machinery, large tools and other expensive items

__ Racks and display fixtures for retail selling areas or trade shows

__ Office furniture—desks, chairs, tables, etc.

__ Leasehold improvements or any alterations you make to the building, including walls, bathrooms and carpeting

__ Purchase of property for business use only (If you purchase a building or warehouse for your business, it may be considered a capital expenditure.)

__ Computers and computer systems, software, copy machines, printers, credit card processing terminal, fax machines, adding machines, cash registers, telephone systems and other small equipment you purchase for your business

A Typical Capital Items Checklist, cont'd

___ Initial or starting inventory

___ Lease deposits

___ Tax deposits

___ Business licenses and permits

___ Opening marketing and promotional materials, including advertising

___ Insurance

___ Telephone installation

___ Utility deposits

___ Office supplies and stationery

___ Legal fees, costs to incorporate or file a Doing Business As (DBA) notice and CPA fees to establish your business

___ A contingency reserve for as many months as you need to begin showing a monthly profit

Your capital spending plan should reflect costs as accurately as possible.

"The cash flow spreadsheet is probably the most important financial statement in the business plan; the cash flow forecast really emphasizes that cash is king and shows you how your money will be going in and out of the business on a month-to-month basis. That's what banks want to look at when making a loan; they want to make sure the cash flow will service the payments over the term of the loan."

Curtis Roeschley
Director
Jane Addams Hull House Association—Small Business Development Center
Chicago, IL

Example of a Capital Spending Estimate for a Product Business		Example of a Capital Spending Estimate for a Service Business	
Item	Amount	Item	Amount
Manufacturing costs for initial inventory	$10,000	Computer, printer, software	$ 5,000
Leasehold improvements, including signs, lights, office build-outs	$35,000	Fax machine and copier	$ 3,000
Rent deposit—2 months' rent	$15,000	Telephone system	$ 1,000
Telephone and computer equipment	$12,000	Desk, conference table, chairs	$ 3,500
Warehousing for initial inventory	$ 7,000	Association fees, dues	$ 1,500
Contingency funds	$25,000	Contingency funds	$10,000
Stationery, supplies	$ 1,000	Stationery, supplies	$ 1,000
Deposits for utilities, business license, incorporating	$ 1,500	Deposits for utilities, business license, incorporating	$ 1,500
Opening marketing, advertising and PR	$ 3,000	Opening marketing, advertising and PR	$ 3,000
Total capital needed to open	$110,500	Total capital needed to open	$29,500

Develop a Cash Flow Forecast

Once you have determined how much money you will need to open your doors, plan out how much cash flow you estimate you will take in each month and determine how quickly your business will start showing a monthly profit.

Calculating a cash flow forecast will help you determine how much investment is required to start your business, and it will also highlight potential problem months. Complete the cash flow worksheet to forecast the first 2 years of your business. Note: If any of your figures are losses, place brackets around them or change the color to red. This will effectively show where trouble spots may be occurring. Once you have your cash flow forecast complete, compare it each month with your actual cash flow to see how accurately you forecasted and to pinpoint months that may need additional promotion to increase sales.

Complete the following Cash Flow Forecast worksheet.

Cash Flow Forecast													
Month	1	2	3	4	5	6	7	8	9	10	11	12	Year Total
Profit/Loss													
Less: Credit sales													
Plus: Collections of credit sales													
Plus: Credit purchases													
Less: Payments for credit purchases													
Plus: Withholding ___ % of total wages													
Less: Quarterly withholding payments													
Plus: Depreciation													
Less: Principal payments													
Less: Extra purchases													
Other cash items in/(out)													
Monthly net cash													
Cumulative net cash													

Note: A Partial Cash Flow Statement worksheet can be viewed in Chapter 20: Planning Worksheets.

Accounting and Bookkeeping

Few entrepreneurs are trained accountants, but the successful ones let the numbers lead them. Before you devise marketing or financial strategies or make most everyday decisions, always ask, "What is the bottom line?" Answers will surface if you maintain accurate and complete financial records. To keep good financial records, you do not need an accounting degree. You just need to be organized, diligent and accurate with mathematical calculations.

Start by opening a separate checking account for your business with your company's name, address and phone number printed on the checks. To open a company bank account, you need to obtain an employer identification number for your company. To obtain this, simply file Form SS-4 with the Internal Revenue Service. If you are a corporation, you may be required to produce a corporate resolution duly signed—often with the corporate seal—as an official corporate indication of authorization to open such an account. Write checks for every business-related purchase and deposit all income into your business checking account. Balance your account at least monthly, and keep all canceled checks on file for at least 3 years, as required for IRS tax audits. To keep track of expenditures, never make checks out to Cash.

> **There is a distinction between accounting and bookkeeping procedures.**
>
> **Accounting**—A beginning-to-end process of collecting financial data, generating financial statements and preparing tax forms.
>
> **Bookkeeping**—The function of collecting financial data only.

Most small business owners are not knowledgeable in bookkeeping and accounting procedures, and this is usually the first area that is outsourced.

The two basic accounting methods are cash and accrual.

Cash Method

This is the accounting method used by individuals and many small businesses. Due to its simplicity, it may be appropriate for your small business. Determining gross income with the cash method is merely a matter of adding up the cash, checks and fair market value of property and services you receive during the year. In other words, you record income at the time cash is received and record the expense when you make the payment. Using this method, your income for the year includes all checks you receive regardless of when you cash the checks or withdraw the money. You cannot avoid paying tax by not depositing checks or credit card charge slips.

Using the cash method, your business expenses are usually deducted in the year you pay them. For example, you order some office supplies from a mail-order catalog in November, and they arrive in December. You send a check to pay for them in January of the following year. Under the cash method, that business deduction should be claimed on the following year's tax return because that is the year you paid for the supplies.

Certain businesses cannot use the cash method. The IRS requires you to declare the accounting method you will use, and if your corporation's annual average gross receipts exceed $5 million, you must use the accrual method. Smaller businesses with few credit accounts most often use the cash method of accounting. Special rules apply for the accounting of inventory. See IRS Publication 538 "Accounting Periods and Methods" for more information.

Accrual Method

This method of accounting is more precise than the cash method. Its main purpose is to match income and expenses in the correct year. With the accrual method, you record a transaction at the time it is made regardless of when the payment occurs. For example, the accrual method calls for you to report income for the year when you perform a service for a customer. It does not matter that your customer does not pay you until the following year. If you keep sales inventory, it is generally preferable to use accrual accounting.

Similarly, you generally deduct your business expenses in the year you become liable for them regardless of when you actually pay them. Under the accrual method, you can deduct the business expenses for office supplies on your tax return for the year in which you ordered the supplies and they were delivered. Even if you paid for them the following year, you can deduct the expenses in the year in which you became liable for them.

Once you decide which accounting method is the right one for your business, you must follow it consistently. Generally, you cannot change your method of accounting unless you get special permission from the IRS.

Bookkeeping

Basic accounting involves six ledgers: income, expense, payroll, inventory, credit and equipment depreciation. Make an entry in the appropriate ledger for each transaction, including date, description and amount. Tally monthly and yearly totals and then store them in a safe, fireproof place.

For each income ledger entry, you must distinguish between business and nonbusiness income. Business income is money generated through the sale of products or services. Nonbusiness income is raised by means unrelated to your business activity, such as a partner contribution, bank interest or loan repayment. Also distinguish between taxable and nontaxable sales and record all sales tax collected. Sales volume determines how often you post income and what proof of purchase you use—either detailed cash register printouts or your suppliers' dated, numbered and signed invoices. Be sure to file voids and returns separately.

The expense ledger includes about a dozen categories, including inventory, payroll, supplies, rent and taxes. Tailor your ledger to account for your major expense categories. How you earn money is as important as how you spend it. For each purchase you make, obtain a copy of the invoice or receipt. Stamp "Posted" on the invoice as you enter it in your ledger. Write the check number on each paid invoice and stamp it "Paid." If you see a need to set aside petty cash for expenses too small to write a check for, make out one check payable to Cash for $20 to $50. Keep the cash in a safe place with an informal slush fund ledger that lists name, date, purpose and amount of each withdrawal.

Under the payroll category in the expense ledger, include net pay and withheld payroll taxes at the time you pay them. Use a separate payroll ledger to break down all other detailed costs.

Plan Your Personnel

> ### Include a description of your staffing schedule:
>
> • How many people will you need to staff the business each day?
>
> • What are the titles of each person hired?
>
> • How many total staffing hours are needed each week?
>
> • What are the hours each person will work?

> ### Write a job description for each employee. Each job description should include job and education requirements:
>
> • Job title
>
> • Job duties
>
> • Skills required, personality desired
>
> • Education requirements
>
> • Language requirements—English speaking, multilingual
>
> • Who will be their immediate supervisor
>
> • Citizenship requirements
>
> • Pay rate and monthly total wages/salary, including benefits

Payroll Projections and Planning Salary Increases

As part of your budget planning process, include a detailed payroll forecast. An example form can be found on the Web landing page www.socrates.com/books/business-plan.aspx.

Payroll by Classification by Month

Salaried and Hourly Labor

Break out how much you will be spending each month for salaried and hourly employee help.

Casual labor is a term derived from some state employment agencies. It refers to any type of work that does not promote or advance the business of the employer. Casual labor has no federal employment tax significance. Seasonal help is often needed for sporting events, holidays, commercial fishing or harvest seasons. Whether you are getting paid or paying someone else, questions often arise over the tax treatment of payments for casual labor, temporary help and seasonal help.

Casual or seasonal employees are subject to the same tax withholding rules that apply to other employees. Employers are required to collect Social Security information and file a Form 1099 for any casual labor employee who has earned more than $600 during the year from a single employer.

Contract Laborer/Independent Contractors

Similar to a contract laborer, an independent contractor is self-employed, bears responsibility for his or her own taxes and expenses and is not subject to an employer's direction and control. Terms of employment are defined with a start and finish date.

Benefit Costs

Along with your employment costs, include the cost of any benefits provided to an employee. If you are providing health benefits, parking reimbursement or travel costs, itemize each benefit and assign a monetary value to it every month to track total personnel expenses.

Using Your Business Plan to Get a Loan

"When presenting your plan to investors or bankers, you can predict the range of questions you will likely receive. Example: If an investor has a financial background, they will ask questions about the revenue plan, profitability and the cash cycle of the business, among other things. They will need to know the marginal economics of the business. For every incremental dollar or unit sold, they will want to know how it impacts the change in profitability of the company and the reinvestment requirement in working capital and capital expenditures. Each business and each prospective stakeholder is different. Each investor will need an education."

William Lederer
Chairman & CEO
Minotaur Capital Management
Chicago, IL

Financing Your Business

Your goal should be to finance your startup with as little of your own money as possible. That way you have money in reserve in case you underestimate your costs or need it in an emergency. Interest on most business loans is tax-deductible. Leverage allows you to build your business today so it can stand on its own two feet tomorrow.

When shopping for credit, aim for the longest terms, the lowest interest rate and the least collateral and personal liability as possible. You may choose fixed, lump sum, periodic or balloon payments. Prioritize them according to your specific needs. In the financing section of your business plan, be sure to detail the interest rate, terms and conditions you desire. Carefully plan your cash flow statement as accurately as possible. Negotiate payments to coincide with both short- and long-term income projections. This requires planning and discipline. Worst-case cash flow scenarios are safer and more realistic—what is the least amount of money you will make? Time the opening of your company for approximately a month before peak season. Promote your venture well in advance. Make sure you have the right to pay off the loan before it is due without being charged a prepayment penalty, which is illegal in many states.

When seeking to obtain money, start with family, friends, business associates, suppliers (see Innovative Financing) and retailers. Typically, those most familiar with you and your business are most willing to back you. Be sure to get all terms and conditions in writing. A promissory note outlines the interest, payment plan, terms and conditions of the loan. Sign the original and mark Copy on the duplicate you file. Regardless of the source, guarantees and promissory notes should always accompany borrowed money to avoid disputes.

Other Sources of Loans

You need capital to pay for your company location and equipment, maintain supplies and operations, market and deliver your product, and recruit and keep employees.

> "How much risk is too much risk? Write down the dollar figure your are willing to risk. If you think you might pass out once you put the figure on paper, then it is too much. If you write down the figure and there is no pain at all, it's probably too little. Understand your own financial situation. What you can risk also means what you can lose. This is not a matter of that you do not risk and everyone else does. Investors do not like to hear you're not putting in any of your own money, and yet you expect them to take a financial risk."
>
> **Sara Shifrin**
> **Director of Entrepreneur Training**
> **Women's Business Development Center**
> **Chicago, IL**

Here are several sources of financing:

Banks–For a small business, look to a community bank. Build a relationship with your banker by utilizing the bank's products and soliciting advice. Today, banks are more conservative than ever when lending money, but once they do, they will work with you to succeed.

Finance Companies–These are easier than banks for getting loans, but they usually charge higher rates and have no vested interest in your success.

Credit Cards–These can help you maintain cash flow in the short term, but beware—credit card rates and terms are volatile, and you can ruin your credit rating by overusing them.

Investors–Whether friends, family or investment firms, investors can provide you upfront cash for a share of future profits. They may also want to share in, or at least monitor, your operations. A good source for finding investors is to join trade associations in the markets in which you intend to sell.

Grants–Visit the Web site of the Small Business Administration–<u>www.sba.gov</u>–for information on small business loans and grants. Also check with your state and local government business development offices as well as educational, research and medical institutions.

Yourself–This is the most important financial source for two reasons.

1. Banks and investors will want to know how much of your own money you are investing in the business.

2. Accumulating your own funds slows you down, and that is a good thing when you are impatient to start getting rich. Patience allows you to accomplish vital homework, market research and planning.

Raise necessary capital by liquidating savings accounts, stocks, bonds and other investments, or by selling a house or other big-ticket items.

Bank Loans

> "The most advantageous form of financing is debt. It's the cheapest. Anything that is a loan will be cheaper than—in most cases—an investment or equity. Debt is always cheaper than equity."
>
> **Kelly Mizeur**
> **Finance Counselor**
> **Women's Business**
> **Development Center**
> **Chicago, IL**

You should approach a commercial bank for a loan only after exhausting all other resources. Typical commercial loans from a bank provide working capital and carry 5-year payback terms with higher interest rates than personal loans. Most states have a limit on the interest rate a bank is allowed to charge on business loans. If you can get it, a line of credit is ideal for covering unexpected expenses as they occur.

Typical institutional lenders invest no more than 50 percent of needed financing. They expect you to cover the rest through personal contributions or some other sources. A substantial personal investment proves your commitment to the venture. The bank will likely put a lien on your company's receivables, inventory and owned equipment. Be careful when pledging personal assets to secure your loan. If your business falters, you may have trouble recovering enough to try again. Even if you form a corporation, the bank may still sue you for nonpledged assets and garnish your wages in order to recover the principal. A loan to an LLC may require a personal guarantee, which also binds shareholders during the startup stages.

Ultimately, loan officers are no more than an extension of the bank. They need to be sure you have a sound and well-researched business plan, broad experience and knowledge, and often more importantly, plenty of collateral.

Pinpoint how large a loan you need with an itemized list of accurately projected upfront expenses, typically for the first 16 months. Asking for slightly more than you need gives you a comfortable cushion, but expenses of more than 15 percent in excess of comparable businesses in your area look suspicious to any intelligent loan officer. If you can establish a line of credit, your company gains access to money whenever it is needed.

Types of Bank Financing

Asset-Based Financing

Asset-based financing is a general term describing a situation where the lender accepts as collateral the assets of a company in exchange for a loan. Generally, asset-based loans are collateralized against accounts receivables, inventory or equipment. Banks will only advance funds on a percentage of receivables or inventory— the typical percentages being 75 percent of receivables or 50 percent of inventory.

Line of Credit

The bank sets aside a predetermined amount of funds for the business to draw against as cash is needed. When funds are used, the credit line is reduced and when payments are made, the line is replenished.

Letter of Credit

A letter of credit is a guarantee from the bank that a specific obligation of the business will be honored. The bank generates its income by charging fees for making the guarantee.

Floor Planning

Floor planning is another form of asset-based lending in which the borrower's inventory is used as collateral for the loan.

"I determine a desirable return on investment before going into a new venture, but I do not try to measure it too continuously. I care about the cost of capital, and during the course of the venture, I think about the firm's projects and whether these earn the cost of capital. How value-added are these individual projects—not whether they generate revenue or profitability but relative to the cost of time and money and relative to all other choices? Is this really the best choice? I measure because I believe in metrics. What can be improved upon systematically is what gets measured. What gets measured gets done. I believe it and know it to be the case."

William Lederer
Chairman & CEO
Minotaur Capital Management
Chicago, IL

SBA Loans

To determine if you qualify for SBA's financial assistance, you should first understand some basic credit factors that apply to all loan requests. Every application needs positive credit merits to be approved. These are the same credit factors a lender will review and analyze before deciding whether to internally approve your loan application, seek a guaranty from SBA to support their loan to you or decline your application altogether.

Small Business Investment Companies

Small Business Investment Companies (SBICs) are privately owned venture capital firms organized under the auspices of the SBA. SBICs lend money to or invest in small businesses primarily within their local area. To find out more, contact your nearby Small Business Development Center. Visit www.sba.gov to find the nearest location.

Certified Development Centers

Another program of the SBA, Certified Development Centers, provide long-term (10- and 20-year) fixed-rate loans for small businesses to finance fixed assets such as real estate—land and buildings. The program is also known as the 504 Loan Program. To find out more call the SBA at 800.827.5722 and inquire about the 504 Loan Program.

Your State's Economic Development Department

Most states have an Economic Development Department that offers a variety of loan programs and services to statewide businesses. Visit your state's Web site to find out about programs in your state.

Angel Investors

Angel investors are individuals, usually ex-entrepreneurs, who seek to increase their net worth and help aspiring entrepreneurs by investing their money and experience to new ventures. Angels come in many forms: some work solo; some look for a piece of the company's ownership by taking an equity stake; others seek only to lend money; and some come in flocks—they belong to investment groups or angel organizations.

Equity Investment

Business loan applicants must have a reasonable amount invested in their business to ensure that it can operate on a sound basis when combined with borrowed funds. Lenders will examine carefully the debt-to-worth ratio of the applicant in order to understand how much money they are being asked to lend–debt–in relation to how much the owners have invested–worth. Owners invest either assets that are applicable to the operation of the business and/or cash which can be used to acquire such assets. The value of invested assets should be substantiated by invoices or appraisals for startup businesses or current financial statements for existing businesses.

Strong equity with a manageable debt level provides financial resiliency to help a firm weather periods of operational adversity. Minimal or nonexistent equity makes a business susceptible to miscalculation and thereby increases the risk of defaulting on borrowed funds. Strong equity ensures the owners remain committed to the business. Sufficient equity is particularly important for new businesses. Weak equity makes a lender more hesitant to provide any financial assistance. However, low equity in relation to existing and projected debt can be overcome with a strong showing in all the other credit factors.

Determining whether a company's level of debt is appropriate in relation to its equity requires analysis of the company's expected earnings and the viability and variability of these earnings. The stronger the support for projected profits, the greater the likelihood the loan will be approved. Applications with high debt, low equity and unsupported projections are prime candidates for loan denial.

Source of Cash Statement

Provide a source of cash statement to any lending institution to show your company's cash potential.

Source of Cash Worksheet	
Business name:	Period covering: Jan. 1 to Dec. 31
1. Cash on hand	
2. Sales (revenues)	
Product income	
Services income	
Deposits on sales or services	
Collections on accounts receivables	
Retainers received on sales or services	
Total sales	$0
3. Miscellaneous income	
Interest income	
Payments to be received on loans	
Total miscellaneous income	$0
4. Sale of long-term assets	$0
5. Liabilities	
Loan from lending institutions, investors, SBA, angels, etc.	
Total liabilities	$0
6. Equity	
Owner investments (sole proprietors/partners)	
Contributed capital (corporation)	
Sale of stock (corporation)	
Venture capital	
Total equity	$0
A. Less product sales	$0
Total cash available	$0
B. With product sales	$0

Cash Flow and Income Projections

Cash flow projections are the most important projections because they detail the anticipated cash inflow and outflow. How much capital will you need to finance your startup? This can be difficult to judge, especially before you have a few months' figures to rely on. To ensure that you always have enough cash on hand, your projections need to be as accurate as possible.

For projected expenses, begin with fixed costs including rent, utilities, insurance, equipment and salary. Add variable costs, such as inventory, supplies, production costs and delivery. For projected income, use industry standards and demographic analysis to project how many customers you will draw. Estimate the average price customers will spend on your goods. Take into account the impact of major competitors, the scope of your promotional efforts and the attractiveness of your location. Subtract a quarter of your modest income estimate, as it inevitably takes time to develop customer awareness and loyalty. If expenses outweigh income, you need to rework your plan in order to cut expenses, obtain a loan or conduct a sales promotion to increase income.

> "Be careful what you ask for. If you are not willing to walk away from your company, do not accept venture capital because you are never again in complete control of your company. Unless you are okay with it, raise other kinds of money."
>
> **Kelly Mizeur**
> **Finance Counselor**
> **Women's Business Development Center**
> **Chicago, IL**

The categories to be shown in your cashflow statements—monthly, quarterly and annually—include:

Cash Flow Statement	
Beginning Cash Balance	$
Cash receipts:	
Collection of receivables	$
Interest income	$
Other income	$
Total	**$**
Cash disbursements:	
Accounts payable	$
Direct materials	$
Direct labor	$
Equipment	$
Salaries	$
Rent	$
Insurance	$
Leases	$
Advertising	$
Taxes	$
Other expenses	$
Income tax payments	$
Total	$
Net cash from operations	$
Sale of stock	$
Decrease (or increase) in funds invested (interest)	$
Short-term borrowings (repayments)	$
Ending Cash Balance	$

A major factor in your financing is liquidity, or the ability to pay your bills. Liquid assets include cash and possessions that can be turned into cash readily–such as checks, credit receivables and inventory–some more easily than others. Will you have enough liquid assets to cover all impending bills? To be solvent, you must be able to pay your bills as they fall due. Your assets must exceed your liabilities. The ratio should be at least 2-to-1; 3- or 4-to-1 is safer. A sound practice in initial stages of starting your company is to add cash and other assets while cutting expenses such as your personal salary.

Experience will tell you to add 30 percent to the most generous expense estimate. Then add another 15 percent to the adjusted total for emergencies and other unexpected expenses.

Cash to Be Paid Out Worksheet

Projecting the amount of cash to be paid out is as important as knowing where the cash will come from. This is a sample worksheet to help you calculate your cash expenditures.

Business name:		Period covering: Jan. 1 to Dec. 31
1. Startup costs		$2,600
Business license	$100	
Corporation filing	$1,000	
Legal fees	$1,000	
Other startup costs:	$500	
A.	$0	
B.	$0	
C.	$0	
D.	$0	
2. Inventory purchases		$40,000
Cash out for goods intended for resale		
3. Variable expenses (selling)		
Advertising/marketing/PR	$10,000	
Freight	$2,500	
Fulfillment of orders	$1,000	
Packaging costs	$500	
Sales salaries/commissions	$20,000	
Travel	$2,500	
Miscellaneous	$500	
Total selling expenses		$37,000
4. Fixed expenses (administration)		
Financial administration	$2,000	
Insurance	$1,500	
Licenses and permits	$200	
Office salaries	$15,000	
Rent expense	$10,000	
Utilities	$3,000	

Leasing contracts	$1,000	
Miscellaneous	$500	
Total administrative expense		$33,200
5. Assets (long-term purchases)		
Cash to be paid out in current period		$10,000
6. Liabilities		
Cash outlay for retiring debts, loans and/or accounts payable		$37,000
7. Owner equity		
Cash to be withdrawn by owner/partners		$25,000
Total cash to be paid out		$157,800

Personal Financial Statements

Most lenders require you to project your salary as part of overall expenses. If you agree to a low salary, it proves your willingness to sacrifice immediate personal gain to ensure a profitable venture—especially if you sacrificed a lucrative career to do so. Include with your fiscal projections a record of your personal finances and list each asset you will contribute along with the market value of each.

Can you afford to wait while the company struggles to show a profit? How much equity will you invest in the venture? Complete the worksheet that follows summarizing your personal financial statement.

Personal Financial Statement

Assets

Cash and cash equivalents

Checking and savings accounts—include money market accounts

Institution name and location	Account type	Account no.	Current balance
1			
2			
3			

Total checking and savings $_____

Time deposit accounts—including CDs

Institution name and location	Account type	Account no.	Current balance	Maturity date
1				
2				
3				

Total deposits $_____

Miscellaneous cash on hand

Institution name and location	Account type	Account no.	Current balance
1			
2			

Total deposits $_____

Marketable securities

Institution name and location	Account type	Account no.	Current balance
1			
2			

Total Value $_____

Cash value of life insurance

Policy holder	Policy type	Policy no.	Cash value
1			
2			

Total cash surrender value $_____

Trusts, deeds and mortgages	Description	
1		
2		
	Total	$_____ ___
Real estate		
1		
2		
	Total holdings	$_____ ___
Other assets		
1		
2		
	Total assets	$_____ ___

Profit and Loss Statement

Complete monthly and yearly profit and loss statements by combining expense and income ledgers. Under income, leave out sales tax and nonbusiness income. Subtract net inventory used–the amount you started with plus purchases made minus current stock–to determine your gross profit. Subtract all other operating expenses, except sales tax and any nondeductible expenses, to determine net profit. Refer to your accounting ledgers and profit and loss statements frequently to find trends–such as slow sales cycles, overspending and stock shrinkage–that you need to account for to survive.

Profit and Loss Forecast

Month	1	2	3	4	5	6	7	8	9	10	11	12	Total
Sales revenue	$0	$0	$0	$0	$0	$0	$0	$0	$0	$0	$0	$0	$0
Cost of sales													
(Percent of sales)													
Gross profit*	$0	$0	$0	$0	$0	$0	$0	$0	$0	$0	$0	$0	$0
(Percent of sales)													
Fixed expenses:													
Wages/Salaries													
Payroll tax													
Rent/Lease													
Equipment leases													
Marketing & advertising													
Insurance													
Accounting													
Interest expense													
Depreciation													
Utilities													
Telephone													
Supplies													
Bad debts													
Freight													
Miscellaneous													
Total fixed expenses	$0	$0	$0	$0	$0	$0	$0	$0	$0	$0	$0	$0	$0
Profit/Loss**	$0	$0	$0	$0	$0	$0	$0	$0	$0	$0	$0	$0	$0

*Gross profit is calculated by subtracting cost of sales from sales revenue
**Profit/Loss is calculated by subtracting total fixed expenses from gross profit

Balance Sheet Pro Forma

Balance sheets provide an accurate picture of your company's financial health at any one particular time. They show what your company owns and owes and how much it is worth at a certain date. They list the assets you need to support your company; the liabilities listed show how the assets are financed. It is suggested that as a new company you create a balance sheet each month or at least quarterly.

The balance sheet is a simple mathematical form showing assets minus liabilities to equal net worth. The following are the basic categories you should include in your balance sheet pro formas:

Balance Sheet	
Assets:	
Current Assets:	
Cash	$_____
Investments	$_____
Accounts receivable (minus bad debt accounts)	$_____
Notes receivable	$_____
Inventory	$_____
Prepaid expenses	$_____
Total Current Assets	$_____
Fixed Assets:	
Land	$_____
Buildings	$_____
Equipment	$_____
Total Fixed Assets	$_____
Other assets	$_____
Total Assets	$_____
Liabilities and Stockholder's Equity:	
Current liabilities	$_____
Short-term debt	$_____
Accounts payable	$_____
Taxes payable	$_____
Income taxes payable	$_____
Accrued liabilities	$_____
Total Current Liabilities	$_____
Long-term debt	$_____
Stockholder's earnings (deficit)	$_____
Total	$_____
Total Liabilities and Stockholder's Equity	$_____

Pro Forma Cash Flow Statement

Company name

Month	Jan	Feb	Mar	Apr	May	Jun	6-Month period	Jul	Aug	Sep	Oct	Nov	Dec	12-Month period
Beginning cash balance														
Cash receipts														
A. Sales/revenues														
B. Receivables														
C. Interest income														
D. Sales of long-term assets														
Total cash available														
Cash payments														
A. Cost of goods to be sold														
1. Purchases														
2. Material														
3. Labor														
Total cost of goods														
B. Variable expenses														
1. Advertising														
2. Freight														
3. Fulfillment of orders														

4. Packaging costs										
5. Sales/salaries										
6. Travel										
7. Misc. Expenses										
Total variable expenses										
C. Fixed expenses										
1. Financial admin										
2. Insurance										
3. License/permits										
4. Office salaries										
5. Rent expenses										
6. Utilities										
7. Misc. Fixed expenses										
Total fixed expenses										
D. Interest expense										
E. Federal income tax										
F. Other uses										
G. Long-term asset payments										
H. Loan payments										
I. Owner payments										
Total cash paid out										
Cash balance/deficiency										
Loans to be received										
Equity deposits										
Ending cash balance										

Break-Even Point

A break-even chart is often used for startup companies to measure how long the company's total sales will equal total costs. By determining your break-even point, you are showing prospective investors that you know exactly how much money your company will need to begin turning a profit.

Break-even analysis, as it is called, is used to determine how soon your income will cover your startup costs. You can also gauge the sales thrust necessary to make new products viable. Take total fixed costs—rent, utilities, insurance, etc. Divide this by the unit selling price minus variable cost per unit—supplies, labor, marketing, etc. Higher net profit means fewer items you need to sell.

$$\frac{\text{Total Fixed Costs}}{\text{Unit Selling Price–Variable Unit Cost}} = \text{Break-Even Point}$$

Growth Projections

Lenders like to see the potential for growth in their investment. What areas for growth do you see in your industry? Do you plan to enter new markets or expand your product line? How much do you plan to invest in research and development? What share of the market will you command in the future? Outline a sensible 5-year forecast with numbers to accurately support your beliefs.

Monitoring Expenses

To eliminate shrinkage and overspending, administer tight control over all financial transactions. This involves an intricate yet organized system of checks and balances on invoices, inventory, receivables and payroll. Establish an amount–$500, for example–that purchases in excess of which must be approved by a designated company officer. Review, duplicate and keep safe all records for at least 6 years and regularly audit and verify receivables.

"It is better if the business can show a profit sooner rather than later because it is so hard to get money initially. If you can at least show a profitable track record, it may be easier to get money to take the business to the next level."

Sara Shifrin
Director of
Entrepreneur Training
Women's Business
Development Center
Chicago, IL

One expense you must monitor closely is your energy bill. Make sure your bill is not out of line with industry averages readily available through the U.S. Department of Energy. Your utility company may conduct a free survey and suggest ways to help you operate more efficiently. Also, keep long distance phone bills in check. Restrict its use to business calls and hold employees accountable by assigning each person a personal access number and reviewing bills monthly.

Safeguards—Setting Up Checks and Balances

An important but often overlooked aspect of setting up accounting procedures is designing a system of checks and balances to ensure your finances are protected. Spell out in your business plan how you plan to create an accounting system of checks and balances. Carefully consider who will be authorized to sign the checks. Provide a contingency plan in the event the designated check signer is not available. As a backup, assign check writing capabilities to two key employees with the provisions that they both must co-sign the check and they can sign checks only up to a maximum amount. Determine how often your books will be audited and by whom—an outside firm, an independent auditor? State who within the organization has the highest spending power and what that limit is. If the company has multiple partners, outline your process for making purchasing decisions. Thinking through all these important issues now will safeguard your company's financial health.

Evaluating Financial Ratios

Determining various financial ratios provides you with a measuring tool that enables you to see how your company is measuring up. Financial ratios generally fall into three categories:

1. Measures the company's ability to meet short-term obligations.

2. Measures the company's ability to meet long-term obligations.

3. Measures the strength and vigor of the company's health.

Current Ratio

Determine your company's current ratio by looking at the balance sheet and dividing current assets by total current liabilities.

$$\text{Current Ratio} = \frac{\text{Current Assets}}{\text{Current Liabilities}}$$

Example:

Current assets of $100,000 divided by current liabilities of $40,000 is a 2.5-1 ratio. Keep in mind that current ratios are not a precise measurement but a guideline. If your company falls below a 1-1 ratio, your company is in danger of not being able to meet your current liabilities. Staying above a 2-1 ratio means you have twice as many assets as liabilities. Conversely, you do not want your ratios to be too high either. A high ratio indicates that you may have a lot of excess cash that could be put to work to grow your company.

Quick Ratio

The quick ratio does not include inventory or prepaid expenses as part of your current assets because it is sometimes difficult to turn them back into cash. The goal is to keep your quick ratio above 1.0 by a comfortable margin and consistent with your industry.

$$\text{Quick Ratio} = \frac{\text{Cash} + \text{Investments} + \text{Receivables}}{\text{Current Liabilities}}$$

> **Example**
>
> Current Assets of $75,000 divided by current liabilities of $40,000 reflect a 1.9 quick ratio. Again, you want to keep your quick ratio above a 1.0. If your company falls below a 1-1 ratio, your company is in danger of not being able to meet your current liabilities.

Inventory Turnover

Inventory turnover–how many times you turn over your entire inventory–will tell you how liquid your inventories really are. The ratio divides the cost of goods sold by the average value of your inventories.

$$\text{Inventory Turnover} = \frac{\text{Cost of Goods Sold}}{\text{Inventories}}$$

> **Example**
>
> Cost of goods sold of $250,000 divided by inventories of $55,000 reflects a 4.5 inventory turnover ratio. This means that inventory is turned over 4.5 times per year. Expressed in days, inventory turns over every 81 days.

Using numbers as a benchmark or a way to measure your progress is important to managing your financial health. Continuously forecasting and comparing actuals to your projections lets you know where you are toward meeting your goals. If you are on target, stay the course. If your actual figures vary from your projected figures, it is time to take action to bridge the gaps. If you find you are beating your projections, maybe it is time to expand.

Include the following worksheets pro forma and statements in your financial plan (included in Chapter 20):

• Break Even Analysis	• Personal Financial Statement
• Personal Forecast Annual Income	• Sales Revenue Forecast
• Sources of Cash Worksheet	• Cash Flow Forecast
• 3-year Income Projection	• Profit & Loss Forecast

Inventory Record

To keep controls on your inventory levels, conduct a quarterly inventory examination using the inventory record worksheet.

An Inventory Record Form can be found on the Web landing page www.socrates.com/books/business-plan.aspx.

Pulling It All Together

1. Include a capital spending plan checklist and estimate your capital spending as accurately as possible.

2. Outline your personnel plan.

3. Include a description of your staffing schedule.

4. Write a job description for each employee.

5. Estimate payroll projections and salary increases, including benefit costs, if applicable.

6. Describe the checks and balances safeguards you will set up to monitor expenses.

7. Project inventory turnover rates.
   Include copies of the following worksheets:

   - Sales Revenue Forecast

   - Personal Financial Statement

   - Profit & Loss Statement

   - Balance Sheet Pro Forma

   - Estimated Growth Projections

   - Cash Flow Forecast

   - Sources of Cash Worksheet

   - 3-year Income Projection

   - Profit & Loss Forecast

Section ■ Five

13 The Exit Plan— Planning an Exit Strategy

Overview

What happens when your company succeeds and survival is no longer an immediate issue? Will you capitalize on the success you have built to move to the next logical step, or will the thrills of starting a new business be gone? Many entrepreneurs choose to sell their business after they are up and successfully running. Exit strategies are planned well in advance.

Knowing where you want to be with your company requires planning. Whether it is expansion planning or planning an exit strategy, you need to plan ahead. Successful entrepreneurs will often sell a successful business to fund the next startup. Developing an exit–or liquidity– strategy is an important section of your business plan and will be carefully reviewed by investors before providing funding.

> "I always set a timeline of how long I will give a business to meet my expectations to continue operating or when to begin the exit plan."
>
> **William Lederer**
> **Chairman & CEO**
> **Minotaur Capital**
> **Management**
> **Chicago, IL**

Why Companies Are Sold

Infighting Among Owners

Fighting among small business owners has caused the breakdown and breakup of many successful businesses. Problems may occur if one owner is not devoting an equal amount of time and energy into the business as originally agreed. Family members may also become the cause of tension between partners. For example, if a partner passes away, the inheriting family members may want to become active parts of the business and clash with the way the business was agreed to be run. A company may be sold to relieve the owners of constant bickering.

Negotiate termination and buyout agreements early in your business partnership while everyone is still getting along and tensions are low. A more equitable settlement is possible at these times before the partners/owners are no longer speaking to each other.

Growing Pains Resulting in High Borrowing

Growing by leaps and bounds may also mean growing financial commitments. When companies grow quickly, this may result in increased borrowing—often with personal repayment guarantees. If the amount borrowed becomes more than an owner's personal worth, business decisions may become more difficult since the wrong decision may cost the owner his or her home, retirement income or children's education fund. A company may be sold to relieve the owner of personal debt agreements.

The Company Is Thriving

Some owners believe that the optimum time to sell a company is when it is thriving. Selling a company when the economy is good and the business is performing at peak levels will attract buyers, and the sellers will most likely get the maximum price for the company.

The Market Shifts

Companies are affected by many changes—technology, customer trends and industry trends. Keep your ear to the ground and watch for subtle changes in customer buying behaviors, new products and new technologies that may change the way you develop your product or service, or changes in how customers use your products or services.

Boredom

Entrepreneurs who become bored often see company sales decline. Many entrepreneurs will opt to sell the company and use the money to start an exciting new challenge.

Developing an Exit Strategy

What will your exit strategy be? There is no right or wrong exit strategy for a new company to follow. Each strategy is unique to your own goals. There are a number of exit strategies available to small business owners. They include:

Selling All or Only a Portion of the Business

You may be able to sell all or a portion of the business to a buyer. Review your business profitability carefully to determine where you are making—or possibly losing—money. The losing portion may be a cash drain in your market but may be a good fit for another market. Selling a portion of the company that is draining your resources will free up additional cash to grow the profitable portion of the business.

Passing Your Business on to a Family Member

This is an excellent way to transfer the value of the company to heirs in an effort to minimize estate taxes. Carefully determine the structure of the new company and determine in advance who will run the company.

Taking the Company Public via an Initial Public Offering (IPO)

An IPO is the process whereby a corporation offers its stock to the general public for the first time. The stock is then sold through a stock exchange, and the number of shareholders substantially increases. The complexities of taking a company public are enormous, and it requires a big demand of management's time both leading up to and after the initial offering.

This is a great way to gain liquidity quickly, but be aware—once a company sells stock, it becomes a publicly held company that is subject to shareholder voting and approvals. The company can no longer enjoy the anonymity of a private corporation and all decisions and financial records become public knowledge.

Leveraged Buyout (LBO)

An LBO is a corporate finance method under which a company is acquired by a person or entity using the value of the company's assets to finance its acquisition. This allows for the acquirer to minimize its outlay of cash in making the purchase. An LBO is a method by which a business can seek to take over another company or at least gain a controlling interest in that company.

What is unique about an LBO is that the company that is buying the other business borrows a significant amount of money to pay for the purchase price—usually 70 percent or more of the total purchase price. The debt that is incurred is secured against the assets of the business being purchased. Interest payments on the loan will be paid from the future cash flow of the acquired company.

> **"Every business should have an exit strategy built into it because it can impact the kinds of decisions you will make. If someone wants to sell their business within 5 years, one of the first things they need to do is determine what will make that kind of business saleable. That will give you direction on how that business needs to look at the end, and you then back it up as far as how it needs to look initially."**
>
> **Sara Shifrin**
> **Director of Entrepreneur Training**
> **Women's Business Development Center**
> **Chicago, IL**

Employee Stock Ownership Plan (ESOP)

An ESOP is essentially selling the company to your employees. This is a terrific option when the new owner group is made up of key employees in the business. There are certain tax advantages to ESOPs. Creating an ESOP also adds value to the company, as it gives employees a stake in ownership in the company.

Liquidity

This is simply ceasing the operation of the business and selling all assets, paying off credits and keeping the proceeds after taxes. This option, while viewed as the easiest and quickest way to generate money, will produce the least amount of return. This is the most common form of liquidation for companies that are formed as sole proprietorships where the income is dependent on the production of one individual.

> **"The choices of how to sell are numerous. If the company is private, it could go public, but the entrepreneur may be the last investor to exit. Another possibility is to sell your business to your employees. This is a good alternative for many small businesses. It is thinking about your people in a different way. It works extremely well for a lot of people. It has for me more than once."**
>
> **William Lederer**
> **Chairman & CEO**
> **Minotaur Capital Management**
> **Chicago, IL**

Being Acquired

Setting Up Your Company for Sale

Getting a business ready for sale takes time and involves a number of stages:

Firm Up Operations

Spend a great deal of time and effort making sure that your company processes are verifiable and transferrable to the new owners. Back up all data and verify that the backup tapes have been backed up properly. Qualify customer information and quantify sales.

Presale

Prepare marketing materials including a description of each product or service you provide. Include a marketing prospectus or annual report about the company's performance and financial statements.

Initial Marketing

Put the word out quietly and confidentially by contacting a few prospective buyers.

Due Diligence

Interested buyers will investigate your company operations to obtain a more thorough understanding of your operations, marketing strategies and the financial health of your company. At this stage, the buyer signs a nondisclosure document stating that they will not divulge, discuss or utilize any information they learn while reviewing your company's information. Due diligence protects your company from information theft by the buying company.

Final Proposal, Negotiation and Close

The final sales price, financing, and other terms are negotiated until an agreement is made; the deal closes and notices are sent to creditors.

Post-Sale

The companies are merged, customers are notified and transition plans are set in motion.

Preparing a Disaster Plan

Disaster planning is often overlooked by many small businesses, but it is important to the success of the company.

Create a disaster plan for each area of your business—finance, marketing, customer service, development, production, etc. Outline how data and operations will be handled in the event of a natural disaster such as a flood, fire, tornado, hurricane or a building disaster such as a roof collapse or major equipment failure.

Backing up Data, Accounting Ledgers

Make a list of all data, accounting ledgers, customer information, etc. to be backed up on a daily basis. Maintain two backup files—one on the premises and a second stored in an accessible, secure area.

Pulling It All Together

1. Describe your ideal exit strategy.

2. Prepare a disaster plan.

   a) Identify which data you should back up.

   b) Determine a backup schedule.

   c) Store backup data in two separate locations.

   d) Test that all data is properly backed up and mirrors your original data.

   e) Prepare for key personnel being incapacitated for any length of time.

Remember to Register

In order to gain access to free forms, dictionaries, checklists and updates, readers must register their book purchase at <u>Socrates.com</u>. An eight-digit Registration Code is provided on the enclosed CD. See page iv for further details.

14 Packaging Your Ideas for Success

Overview

How you package your business plan will help make a favorable impression with potential investors. A well-organized plan will also be easier to follow.

Package for Success—Binding

A working business plan that will be presented to investors looks professional when bound in a spiral notebook. Although a three-ring binder works best for easy updating, it is the least professional. Most copy centers and stationery supply stores offer low-cost spiral binding that may be easily disassembled for removal of old material and reassembled with updated material. You may also purchase binding equipment for a small cost at most office supply stores or by catalog. This small investment will reap big rewards, as your plan will take on the polished, professional look of a larger company.

For plans that you provide to investors or potential lenders, use a nice cover when binding. Depending on the type of business you are starting, be mindful of cover colors. Avoid colors that are loud or signify danger, such as red, or may have a hidden meaning—green, for example, is the color of money. Select neutral colors such as brown, blue or black that will not subliminally conjure up negative images.

> **Hint**
>
> Be sure to include copies of all supporting material with your working plan.

Length

How long should a plan be? It can be as long as you need to tell the complete story. Be clear and concise. A rule of thumb is that a plan should be no longer than 30 to 40 pages, including supporting documents. Potential lenders do not want to sift through volumes of paper to get to the information they need. When writing each section, view it as a summary and provide only the necessary information. Providing too much detail may cause analysis paralysis—or too much information to digest. If your complete plan is longer than 30 to 40 pages, pare it down. You can always keep the more detailed copy for yourself and provide an abbreviated version for investors.

Presentation

Make your plan look neat and presentable—but not slick. If you cannot produce a professional looking package yourself, you may consider hiring a professional service to make it look more polished. However, do not make your presentation look too polished. Lenders and investors are reviewing your plan strictly for text and numbers. Paying a professional to improve the look of the plan may seem frivolous, and investors may worry that you would not use their funding wisely.

Table of Contents

Always include a table of contents in your business plan. It follows the statement of purpose. Make the table of contents detailed enough that an investor may quickly locate any section of the plan. Include in the table of contents the page numbers for all suporting material. A complete table of contents will include the chapter name and subtitle or header included on each page.

Example

Number Each Copy

Make copies for yourself and for each lender you wish to approach. Keep track of copies by numbering them and recording who receives which copy. Limit the number of potential lenders you work with at any one time. If your loan is turned down or an investor states that they are not interested, make sure to get your business plan back. Asking a potential investor to sign a noncompete or nondisclosure agreement protects you from investors who read the plan just to get new ideas.

Copyright Your Plan

Your plan is the culmination of your ideas and hard work. Protect your work from being appropriated by other investors or companies. Always include copyright information in the footer on the bottom of the document. Include the word Copyright or the symbol (©) along with the year it was produced:

Copyright 2005 Socrates Media, LLC.

All rights reserved. This material may not be copied, duplicated or electronically submitted without the written permission of the copyright holder.

Or:

© 2005 Socrates Media, LLC.

All rights reserved. This material may not be copied, duplicated or electronically submitted without the written permission of the copyright holder.

You may also include a written disclaimer for added protection:

> This Business Plan has been prepared by the management team of Company A and is being furnished to select individuals for the sole purpose of providing financing to the Company. This Business Plan is a confidential document that contains ideas, concepts, methods and other proprietary information. Readers are to treat the information contained herein as confidential and may not copy any of these materials without the written permission of the creator.

Nondisclosure Agreement

A nondisclosure agreement (NDA) or confidential disclosure agreement (CDA) is a legal contract between two parties that outlines confidential materials that the parties wish to share with each other for certain purposes but wish to restrict from generalized use.

NDAs are commonly signed when two companies or individuals are considering doing business together and need to understand the technology or processes used in each other's businesses solely for the purpose of evaluating the potential business relationship. NDAs can be mutual, meaning both parties are restricted in their use of the materials provided, or they can restrict only a single party.

It is also possible for an employee to sign an NDA or NDA-like agreement with a company at the time of hiring; in fact, some employment agreements will include a clause restricting confidential information in general.

Some issues related to drafting NDAs include:

- the definition of what is confidential—today's NDAs will typically include a laundry list of the types of items covered, including unpublished patent applications; know-how; schematics; financial information; verbal representations; business strategies, etc.

- provisions restricting the transfer of data in violation of national security

- the term in years of the confidentiality

- the term in years that the agreement is binding

Remember to Register

In order to gain access to free forms, dictionaries, checklists and updates, readers must register their book purchase at Socrates.com. An eight-digit Registration Code is provided on the enclosed CD. See page iv for further details.

A simple nondisclosure agreement might look something like this:

EXAMPLE MUTUAL NONDISCLOSURE AGREEMENT

This Agreement, made as of the last date set forth on the last page hereof (the Effective Date), by and between the Directors of the Company (hereafter Company) and _____, sets forth the terms and conditions of the disclosure and receipt of certain Confidential Information between the parties. The party disclosing Confidential Information, as herein defined, shall be referred to as the Discloser and the party receiving such Confidential Information shall be referred to as the Recipient. The term Confidential Information shall refer to the Confidential Information disclosed by any party to this Agreement.

The parties signing this document agree as follows:

1. Confidential Information may include information that is disclosed to Recipient by Discloser in any manner, whether orally, visually or in tangible form (including without limitation, documents, devices and computer readable media) and all copies thereof. Tangible materials that disclose or embody Confidential Information shall be marked by Discloser as Confidential, Proprietary or the substantial equivalent thereof. Confidential Information that is disclosed orally or visually shall be identified by Discloser as confidential at the time of disclosure and promptly thereafter identified as confidential in a written document provided to Recipient.

2. Except as expressly permitted herein, for a period of 3 years from the effective date (Nondisclosure Period), Recipient shall maintain in confidence and not disclose Confidential Information.

3. Recipient shall have the right to use Confidential Information solely for the purpose(s) specified within this Agreement (Permitted Purpose(s)).

4. Recipient shall disclose Confidential Information only to those of its employees who have a need to know such information for the Permitted Purpose(s).

5. Confidential Information shall not include any information that Recipient can demonstrate:

    i. was in Recipient's possession without confidentiality restriction prior to disclosure by Discloser hereunder;

    ii. was generally known in the trade or business practiced by Discloser at the time of disclosure through no act of Recipient;

    iii. has come into the possession of Recipient without confidentiality restrictions from a third party, and such third party is under no obligation to Discloser to maintain the confidentiality of such information; or

    iv. was developed by Recipient independently of and without reference to Confidential Information.

If a particular portion or aspect of Confidential Information becomes subject to any of the foregoing exceptions, all other portions or aspects of such information shall remain subject to all of the provisions of this Agreement.

6. Recipient agrees not to reproduce or copy by any means Confidential Information, except as reasonably required to accomplish the Permitted Purpose(s). Upon termination of this Agreement, Recipient's right to use Confidential Information, as granted in Paragraph 3 above, shall immediately terminate. In addition, upon such termination, or upon demand by Discloser at any time, or upon expiration of this Agreement, Recipient shall return promptly to Discloser or destroy, at Discloser's option, all tangible materials that disclose or embody Confidential Information; Recipient, however, may retain one copy of Discloser's Confidential Information for archival purposes only.

7. Recipient shall not remove any proprietary rights legend from and shall, upon Discloser's reasonable request, add proprietary rights legends to materials disclosing or embodying Confidential Information.

8. Discloser understands that Recipient develops and acquires technology for its own products and/or internal applications, and that existing or planned technology independently developed or acquired by Recipient may contain ideas and concepts similar or identical to those contained in Discloser's Confidential Information. Discloser agrees that entering this Agreement shall not preclude Recipient from developing or acquiring technology similar to Discloser's without obligations to Discloser, provided that Recipient does not use Confidential Information to develop such technology.

9. Company's Confidential Information will not be introduced in any future products marketed by the other party to this Agreement.

10. Neither party has any obligation under or by virtue of this Agreement to purchase from or furnish to the other party any products or services, or to enter into any other agreement, including but not limited to a development, consulting, purchasing or technology licensing agreement.

11. Other than as expressly specified herein, Discloser grants no license to Recipient under any copyrights, patents, trademarks, trade secrets or other proprietary rights to use or reproduce Confidential Information.

12. Notwithstanding any other provisions of this Agreement, Recipient agrees not to export, directly or indirectly, any U.S. source technical data acquired from Discloser or any products utilizing such data to any countries outside the United States if such export would be in violation of the United States Export Control Laws or Regulations then in effect.

13. The interpretation, application and enforcement of this Agreement shall be governed by the laws of the State of _____ without reference to choice of law principles. Any claim, suit or cause of action involving the interpretation, application or enforcement of this Agreement shall be commenced in Company's County and State of choice.

14. This Agreement expresses the entire agreement and understanding of the parties with respect to the subject matter hereof and supersedes all prior oral

or written agreements, commitments and understandings pertaining to the subject matter hereof. Any modifications of or changes to this Agreement shall be in writing and signed by both parties.

15. Unless earlier terminated in accordance with the provisions hereof, this Agreement shall remain in full force and effect for the duration of the Nondisclosure Period, whereupon it shall expire. Either party may terminate this Agreement at any time, without cause, effective immediately upon written notice of termination; however, in the event this Agreement is terminated prior to expiration of the Nondisclosure Period, its provisions shall survive and remain in effect for the remainder of the Nondisclosure Period, with respect to Confidential Information disclosed prior to the effective date of termination.

PERMITTED PURPOSES

A. The Permitted Purpose with respect to Confidential Information disclosed to Company shall be a presentation/discussion on:

B. The Permitted Purpose with respect to Confidential Information disclosed to Recipient shall be:

CONFIDENTIAL DISCLOSURE

A. Company identifies the following as its Confidential Information to be disclosed hereunder:

B. Recipient identifies the following as its Confidential Information to be disclosed hereunder:

RECIPIENT

By: _____

Signature: _____

Title: _____

Date: _____

COMPANY

By: _____

Signature: _____

Title: _____

Date: _____

Pulling It All Together

1. Neatly package your plan for visual appeal and ease of use.

2. Include support material with your plan.

3. Number each copy.

4. Retrieve all copies from noninterested investors.

5. Include a copyright statement on each page.

6. Create a nondisclosure agreement form.

Learning the Language of Business

Readers are entitled to full access and use of the comprehensive Business Law and Accounting & Finance Dictionaries found on the Web landing page at www.socrates.com/books/business-plan.aspx. Please remember to register the first time you use this free resource. See page iv for instructions.

15 Keep It Current

Overview

Putting your plan together is hard work. You spent hours laboring over facts, figures, plans, worksheets and schematics. Your plan is now the roadmap to a successful business venture. Keep it nearby and refer to it at least once a month. It is a living, breathing document that will change many times during the course of a year. Embrace the changes but always keep your mission and goals in mind as you do.

> "A business plan is not a static document. It will constantly be revisited. Do not make this document so heavy or so long so that you are not willing to look at it to see what needs to be revised. The business plan is always about the future, so work toward the future and learn from the past."
>
> **Sara Shifrin**
> **Director of Entrepreneur Training**
> **Women's Business**
> **Development Center**
> **Chicago, IL**

Making Revisions

Every plan will evolve. No matter how thoroughly you initially plan, change happens. Either industry trends change, technology improves or the market changes. As the world around you changes, so must your plan. Changes come in many different forms:

Changes within the Company

- Change of focus—Your business evolves into a new direction brought upon by market or industry changes.

- Diversification—You may decide to diversify your company by purchasing a competitor, entering a new market or finding a new, profitable niche.

- Consolidation—Your industry may be experiencing a trend of consolidation. Companies may be merging with their competitors or the need for your product or service may be shrinking.

- Reorganization—Your company may be experiencing a reorganization of management functions or roles.

> "Most people create a business plan for the purpose of procuring financing from an investor or bank, then put it away. My team and I continuously review our business plan. Plans need to be built bottom up, not top down. They need to be owned across the organization. They need to be revisited. They need to be living, breathing and available. Everybody in the company should see them. And you should not be afraid to revisit them."
>
> **William Lederer**
> **Chairman & CEO**
> **Minotaur Capital Management**
> **Chicago, IL**

Accommodating Customer Changes

Customers may also be experiencing changes in their needs and wants. Frequently reviewing for changes in customer trends will help you:

- institute changes in customer trends and buying patterns; and
- adapt to changes in the industry.

Accepting Technological Changes

Your industry may be experiencing technological changes:

- changes in quality, economy and industry
- cost changes as technology gets cheaper

Implement Changes in Your Business Plan

Frequently review your plan for modifications. Divide the plan review into areas of division–give each person responsible for each area the authority to make suggestions. Make each division or department responsible for its own changes. For an honest opinion, hire an outside consultant to review and recommend changes.

Anticipate Your Problems

Problems or obstacles occur in every business plan. If you discover a discrepancy while working on your plan, develop an alternate plan and budget–a worst-case scenario, if you will–and create a backup plan for product and/or service offerings. For example, when sales are strong, focus on selling a full product or new or replacement equipment. If sales begin to soften, switch to offering repairs or upgrades instead of entire systems or programs.

Planning for Years Ahead

Writing the plan is a large-scale undertaking. However, once you finish creating the plan, keep it up-to-date for future borrowing and growth. Periodically review your plan and make changes as necessary.

Pulling It All Together

1. Create a review calendar. Review your plan at predetermined intervals to update the plan as needed.

2. Develop a worst-case scenario plan and budget.

Section ■ Six

16 Tips for Writing the Best Business Plan

Overview

Where do you begin? Writing a comprehensive business plan may prove overwhelming for some entrepreneurs. Here are a 20 tips to get you started:

1. Write a little at a time—writing just a few sentences is a great start. Get your thoughts on paper and let someone you trust read them. Sometimes talking with a person who is not involved in the business can produce very good ideas.

2. As you put your ideas down on paper, do not worry about format. You can organize your plan after you have assembled all the components. A good business plan must contain certain elements–the executive summary is a must–but the logic in the plan and believable financial projections are the most important parts. If the numbers do not work, no amount of beautiful presentation will make your plan a good one.

3. Do not write a book. Whenever possible, use charts, tables and graphs to present and analyze information. A picture is truly worth a thousand words.

4. Include key components in the business plan. You should have specific goals and develop realistic strategies to meet those goals in a variety of areas: financial, business growth, market share, employment goals, etc. Goals and strategies will appear in your plan briefly at the beginning and in the body, both to express your vision of future business and as the foundation of your financial projections.

   - The mission statement should answer the question: Why are you in business? Your mission should be a concise statement of the primary goals of the business and how these will be achieved. Often it reflects a personal philosophy.

- Your goals are concise statements of what your business will set out to do and when the goal will be achieved. Goals are time-based and measurable—most importantly, goals must be achievable.

- The strategies you use will show how you will meet your goals and who will be responsible. Strategies tell the reader what method you will use to meet your goals. You may have multiple strategies to reach a single goal and strategies may overlap among goals.

5. Build a well-connected team. In seeking equity money from venture capitalists or other outside investors, you will increase your chances of success if you get someone committed to your management team who, if not known personally by a potential investor, at least will have a recognizable name. If that is not possible, consider getting one or more people on your board of directors with whom potential investors may be familiar.

6. Keep track of any public relations. Include as exhibits to your plan any positive media clippings you can find about members of your management team, such as items from trade publications. If you do not have any clippings, contact industry or local publications to get media coverage—perhaps about your startup business proposal.

7. Keep the tone of your business plan factual—avoid using hyperbole or generalizations. Investors and lenders are turned off by statements like: This business has incredible potential. They want to use the more factual information you present to reach their own conclusions.

8. Keep your plan clear and concise. Whether creating a business plan to raise money or an annual plan to run your business, keep it succinct. Avoid providing too much detail as you develop your plan. If a business plan is too long, readers might only skim it. If an annual plan is too long, readers might not focus on what is really important.

9. Involve everyone. Ask key employees to create their area budgets and then work with them until you are satisfied. Have key people get together to get the plan in sync and to get any disagreements out in the open. The more input people have in creating the plan, the more responsibility they will feel toward it.

10. Annual plans are not just budgets. Review your plan for growth and ideas, not just for the numbers. While you do need to use them to run a business, numbers alone lead to a shallow plan. Companies that are run just by the numbers lose direction, drift from their strategy and never realize their full potential. It is essential to the planning process that you articulate clearly what the direction of the company will be for the coming year and the role each person will play in supporting the direction of the company overall.

11. Use your business plan to improve performance. Meet with key people at least once a month to review how your company is performing relative to the plan. This is a great time to review projected numbers against actual results and to keep an eye on new and existing competition.

12. Find a mentor who has complete faith in you and your business idea—someone who is already stable and established, not an overnight success. A good mentor will already have experienced business success, will have been through a lot of ups and downs, and can offer useful advice on what not to do when developing your business. This alone could save you thousands of dollars.

13. Have your business plan drawn up for free by submitting it to an MBA class. Most MBA students are required to take a class on devising complete business plans. This will give you insight into any loopholes you may have overlooked when drafting your original plan. Pinpointing these errors early could save you money in the long run and will also help you be better organized and prepared for the future.

14. Barter strengths with other business owners. Start networking with other small-business owners by joining your city's chamber of commerce or other local business group. At the networking events, do not be shy—ask questions. What are the needs these other businesses have? How are they struggling with different aspects of running and growing their companies? Pinpoint the areas in which they need help and creatively offer those services of your business that can enhance theirs. In exchange, propose that they provide you with help in their area of expertise.

15. Get low- or no-cost advice from a university-affiliated Small Business Development Center. These centers, which are sponsored by the U.S. Small Business Administration and are scattered throughout the country, offer free advice and free or inexpensive workshops to new companies. They provide resources and information regarding every aspect of business. More often than not, entrepreneurs are creative people with great products, but they are lacking skills in some of the other, not so exciting areas of business. Services at these centers include such things as 1-day seminars on getting started, free one-on-one counseling, legal clinics, online resources and downloadable forms.

16. Give the illusion of having more than one location by renting office space on an hourly basis. Why pay monthly rent for office space when you are just starting out? Instead, employ a pay-as-you-use approach. Do most of your work out of your home office. When meeting prospective business associates or clients, rent office or meeting space by the hour.

17. Hire a virtual secretary. Most small-business owners are so busy multi-tasking their primary responsibilities that keeping on top of the small stuff–like answering the phone–can be a challenge. Most new business owners set up voice mailboxes to answer their calls, but this can result in a major loss in business. In a world full of new technology, customers appreciate personal attention. Impatient and demanding, they want to hear a human voice on the other end of the line—someone who can answer their questions or take their order immediately. Remember, if you do not answer, someone else will.

Hiring a virtual secretary also provides the illusion of a professional office atmosphere, even if you are just working out of your den. Virtual secretaries can do anything from setting up appointments and taking messages to answering frequently asked questions. They can even answer your calls 24 hours a day, 7 days a week. Hiring a virtual secretary could cost you as little as $40 a month to start—a small price to pay for excellent customer service.

18. Hire college interns to help with the small tasks. When you are just starting out, it is critical that you focus on the things that will bring in the business—developing your marketing strategies, perfecting your sales skills, performing the work your customers expect from you. But if you are going to find success, you will not have time to do it all. Interns can help out by running errands, making copies or helping with mailings. They can also be trained to answer customers' initial questions about your product or service or handle public relations duties or Web design—it will depend on the expertise of the students you hire. By hiring smart, you can carve out the time you need to deal with bigger and better things.

19. Enlist the help of your support network. When you start a business, it is imperative that you enlist the help and support of people you trust. It is easy for entrepreneurs to get into the mind-set of, "If I need to get something done right, I have to do it myself." While this may be the case, spreading yourself too thin keeps you from building your business properly. In addition, as your business grows, you will not have time to be the janitor, the accountant, the secretary and the chief executive officer.

20. No one knows you better than your family, close friends and partners. Trust that they know your strengths and weaknesses and allow them to help you out by offering complementary assistance. Doing this early on will help you learn to trust that other people can get the job done and will give you practice in the art of management and delegation. Those who believe in you will want to see you succeed, so determine their strengths, get them excited about your vision and ask them to help you out.

Seven Tips to a Successful New Business Launch for a First-Time Entrepreneur:

1. The willingness to be open.
2. The willingness to create a business the way it needs to be created—not the way you would like it to look but the way it needs to look because there are rules to follow.
3. Making sure you are not the center of all this. Making sure you are creating a business that fits a particular market and the type of business you are starting.
4. Making sure you have built in the kind of feedback you need and the number of sales you need each month. You build in the necessary feedback so that you can change as you go along when you do get feedback.
5. Believing in the business plan to the point that you are willing to follow it and look at it. Too many people finish it and breathe a sigh of relief and put it in a drawer and forget about it.
6. Believing in it means knowing up front that it may be totally off base, but you are willing to go ahead with it and willing to change if need be.
7. The willingness to seek help. The business plan gives someone the ability to get help. If everything is in your head, you cannot get help very easily. You need to share your expertise with others and you do this through your plan.

Sara Shifrin
Director of Entrepreneur Training • Women's Business Development Center
Chicago, IL

Mistakes to Avoid

- Being reactive and not being proactive—you have to be proactive about doing whatever it takes to run a successful business by being aware of your competition, changing markets and new opportunities.

- Underestimating the amount of money and time it takes to start a business—if it is done properly, your business plan helps you determine what you will be doing, how you will do it and how much it will cost. Without that business plan, you might not account for every detail, and you might wind up undercapitalized—and out of business.

- Underestimating the amount of time needed to build up a successful business—of course the time commitment will depend on the type of business you are starting and whether you plan to start it full-time or on the side.

- Failing to enlist professionals who can walk you through startup or failing to utilize all your resources–There are certain things you might be able to figure out on your own–marketing materials, for instance–by reading good books and articles, but you do not want to try to figure out things like how to structure your company–sole proprietorship, corporation, etc., or what licenses and permits to get and so on. Even if you get just a little input from an attorney and an accountant, you are probably better off than if you attempt to think of every legal and tax question on your own.

- Not taking advantage of available help—get free advice from a successful mentor such as a Service Corps of Retired Executives volunteer who has already been through the rough-and-tumble first stages of starting a business.

17 Buying a Franchise

Overview

An important step in the small-business startup process is deciding whether or not to go into business at all. Each year, thousands of potential entrepreneurs are faced with this difficult decision. Because of the risk and work involved in starting a new business, many new entrepreneurs choose franchising as an alternative to starting a new, independent business.

One of the biggest mistakes you can make is to hurry into business, so it is important to understand your reasons for going into business and to determine if owning a business is right for you.

If you are concerned about the risk involved in a new, independent business venture, then franchising may be the best business option for you. But remember that hard work, dedication and sacrifice are essential to the success of any business venture, including franchising.

A franchise typically enables you–the investor or franchisee–to operate a business. By paying a franchise fee, which may cost several thousand dollars or more, you are given a format or system developed by the company–the franchiser–the right to use the Franchiser's name for a limited time and assistance. For example, the Franchiser may help you find a location for your outlet; provide initial training and an operating manual; and advise you on management, marketing or personnel. Some Franchisers offer ongoing support such as monthly newsletters, a toll-free telephone number for technical assistance and periodic workshops or seminars.

While buying a franchise may reduce your investment risk by enabling you to associate with an established company, it can be costly. You may also be required to relinquish significant control over your business while taking on contractual obligations with the Franchiser.

A franchise is a legal and commercial relationship between the owner of a trademark, service mark, trade name or advertising symbol and an individual or group wishing to use that identification in a business. The franchise governs the method of conducting business between the two parties. Generally, a franchisee sells goods or services supplied by the Franchiser or that meet the Franchiser's quality standards.

Franchising is based on mutual trust between the Franchiser and franchisee. The Franchiser provides the business expertise–marketing plans, management guidance, financing assistance, site location, training, etc–that otherwise would not be available to the franchisee. The franchisees bring to the franchise operation the entrepreneurial spirit and drive necessary to make the franchise a success.

There are primarily two forms of franchising:

• Product/trade name franchising   • Business format franchising

In the simplest form of franchising, a Franchiser owns the right to a name or trademark and sells that right to a franchisee. This is known as product/trade name franchising. The more complex form, business format franchising, involves a broader ongoing relationship between the two parties. Business format franchises often provide a full range of services, including site selection, training, product supply, marketing plans and even assistance in obtaining financing.

The following are the components of a typical franchise system. Consider each carefully.

The Cost

In exchange for obtaining the right to use the Franchiser's name and its assistance, you may pay some or all of the following fees:

Initial Franchise Fee and Other Expenses

Your initial franchise fee, which may be nonrefundable, may cost between several thousand and several hundred thousand dollars. You may incur significant costs to rent, build and equip an outlet, to purchase initial inventory and to obtain operating licenses and insurance. You also may be required to pay a grand opening fee to the Franchiser to promote your new outlet.

Continuing Royalty Payments

You may have to pay the Franchiser royalties based on a percentage of your weekly or monthly gross income, even if your outlet had not earned significant income during that time. In addition, royalties usually are paid for the right to
use the Franchiser's name. So even if the Franchiser fails to provide promised support services, you still may have to pay royalties for the duration of your franchise agreement.

Advertising Fees

You may have to pay into an advertising fund. Some portion of the advertising fees may go for national advertising or to attract new franchise owners, but not to target your particular outlet.

Controls

To ensure uniformity, Franchisers typically control how franchisees conduct business. These controls may significantly restrict your ability to exercise your own business judgment. The following are typical examples of such controls:

Site approval

Many Franchisers preapprove sites for outlets. This may increase the likelihood that your outlet will attract customers. The Franchiser, however, may not approve the site you want.

Design or Appearance Standards

Franchisers may impose design or appearance standards to ensure customers receive the same quality of goods and services in each outlet. Some Franchisers require periodic renovations or seasonal design changes. Complying with these standards may increase your costs.

Restrictions on Goods and Services Offered for Sale

Franchisers may restrict the goods and services offered for sale. For example, as a restaurant franchise owner, you may not be able to add popular items to your menu or delete items that are unpopular. Similarly, as an automobile transmission repair franchise owner, you might not be able to perform other types of automotive work, such as brake or electrical system repairs.

Restrictions on Method of Operation

Franchisers may require you to operate in a particular manner. The Franchiser might require you to operate during certain hours, use only preapproved signs, employee uniforms and advertisements, or abide by certain accounting or bookkeeping procedures. These restrictions may impede you from operating your outlet as you deem best. The Franchiser also may require you to purchase supplies only from an approved supplier, even if you can buy similar goods elsewhere at a lower cost.

Restrictions of Sales Area

Franchisers may limit your business to a specific territory. While these territorial restrictions may ensure that other franchisees will not compete with you for the same customers, they could impede your ability to open additional outlets or move to a more profitable location.

Terminations and Renewal

You can lose the right to your franchise if you breach the franchise contract. In addition, the franchise contract is for a limited time; there is no guarantee that you will be able to renew it.

Franchise Terminations

A Franchiser can end your franchise agreement if, for example, you fail to pay royalties or abide by performance standards and sales restrictions. If your franchise is terminated, you may lose your investment.

Renewals

Franchise agreements typically run for 15 to 20 years. After that time, the Franchiser may decline to renew your contract. Also, be aware that renewals need not provide the original terms and conditions. The Franchiser may raise the royalty payments or impose new design standards and sales restrictions. Your previous territory may be reduced, possibly resulting in more competition from company-owned outlets or other franchisees.

Before Selecting a Franchise System

Before investing in a particular franchise system, carefully consider how much money you have to invest, your abilities and your goals. The following checklist may help you make your decision.

Your Investment:

- How much money do you have to invest?
- How much money can you afford to lose?
- Will you purchase the franchise by yourself or with partners?
- Will you need financing and if so, where can you obtain it?
- Do you have a favorable credit rating?
- Do you have savings or additional income to live on while starting your franchise?

Your Abilities:

- Does the franchise require technical experience or relevant education, such as auto repair, home and office decorating or tax preparation?
- What skills do you have? Do you have computer, bookkeeping or other technical skills?
- What specialized knowledge or talents can you bring to a business?
- Have you ever owned or managed a business?

Your Goals:

- What are your goals?
- Do you require a specific level of annual income?
- Are you interested in pursuing a particular field?
- Are you interested in retail sales or performing a service?
- How many hours are you willing to work?
- Do you want to operate the business yourself or hire a manager?
- Will franchise ownership be your primary source of income or will it supplement your current income?
- Would you be happy operating the business for the next 20 years?
- Would you like to own several outlets or only one?

Selecting a Franchise

Like any other investment, purchasing a franchise is a risk. When selecting a franchise, carefully consider factors such as the demand for the products or services, likely competition, the Franchiser's background and the level of support you will receive.

Demand

Is there a demand for a Franchiser's products or services in your community? Is the demand seasonal? For example, lawn and garden care or swimming pool maintenance may be profitable only in the spring or summer. Is there likely to be a continuing demand for the products or services in the future? Is the demand likely to be temporary, such as selling a fad food item? Does the product or service generate repeat business?

Competition

What is the level of competition nationally and in your community? How many franchised and company-owned outlets does the Franchiser have in your area? How many competing companies sell the same or similar products or services? Are these competing companies well established with wide name recognition in your community? Do they offer the same goods and services at the same or lower prices?

Your Ability to Operate a Business

Sometimes franchise systems fail. Will you be able to operate your outlet even if the Franchiser goes out of business? Will you need the Franchiser's ongoing training, advertising or other assistance to succeed? Will you have access to the same or other suppliers? Could you conduct the business alone if you had to lay off personnel to cut costs?

Name Recognition

A primary reason for purchasing a franchise is the right to associate with the company's name. The more widely recognized the name the more likely it will draw customers who know its products or services. Therefore, before purchasing a franchise, consider the following:

- how widely recognized the company's name is and whether it has a registered trademark;

- how long the Franchiser has been in operation;

- if the company has a reputation for quality products or services; and

- if consumers have filed complaints against the franchise with the Better Business Bureau or a local consumer protection agency.

Training and Support Services

Another reason for purchasing a franchise is to obtain support from the Franchiser. What training and ongoing support does the Franchiser provide? How does their training compare with the training for typical workers in the industry? Could you compete with others who have more formal training? What backgrounds do the current franchise owners have? Do they have prior technical backgrounds or special training that helps them succeed? Do you have a similar background?

Franchiser's Experience

Many Franchisers operate well-established companies with years of experience both in selling goods or services and in managing a franchise system. Some Franchisers started by operating their own businesses. There is no guarantee, however, that a successful entrepreneur can successfully manage a franchise system.

Carefully consider how long the Franchiser has managed a franchise system. Do you feel comfortable with the Franchiser's expertise? If Franchisers have little experience in managing a chain of franchises, their promises of guidance, training and other support may be unreliable.

Growth

A growing franchise exposition allows you to view and compare a variety of franchise possibilities. Keep in mind that exhibitors at the exposition primarily want to sell their franchise systems. Be cautious of salespersons who are interested in selling a franchise that you are not interested in.

Before you attend, research what type of franchise best suits your investment limitations, experience and goals. When you attend, comparison shop for the opportunity that best suits your needs and ask questions.

Know How Much You Can Invest

An exhibitor may tell you how much you can afford to invest or that you cannot afford to pass up this opportunity. Before beginning to explore investment options, consider the amount you feel comfortable investing and the maximum amount you can afford.

Know What Type of Business is Right for You

An exhibitor may attempt to convince you that an opportunity is perfect for you. Only you can make that determination. Consider the industry that interests you before selecting a specific franchise system. Ask yourself the following questions:

- Have you considered working in that industry before?
- Can you see yourself engaged in that line of work for the next 20 years?
- Do you have the necessary background or skills?

If the industry does not appeal to you or you are not suited to work in that industry, do not allow an exhibitor to convince you otherwise. Spend you time focusing on those industries that offer more realistic opportunities.

Comparison Shop

Visit several franchise exhibitors engaged in the type of industry that appeals to you. Listen to the exhibitor's presentations and discussions with other interested consumers. Get answers to the following questions:

- How long has the Franchiser been in business?
- How many franchised outlets currently exist? Where are they located?
- How much is the initial franchise fee and any additional startup costs? Are there any continuing royalty payments? How much are they?
- What management, technical and ongoing assistance does the Franchiser offer?
- What controls does the Franchiser impose?

Exhibitors may offer you prizes, free samples or free dinners if you attend a promotional meeting later that day or over the next week to discuss the franchise in greater detail. Do not feel compelled to attend. Rather, consider these meetings as one way to acquire more information and to ask additional questions. Be prepared to walk away from any promotion if the franchise does not suit your needs.

Get Substantiation for Any Earnings Representations

Some Franchisers may tell you how much you can earn if you invest in their franchise system or how current franchisees in their system are performing. Be careful. The Federal Trade Commission (FTC) requires that Franchisers making such claims provide you with written substantiation. Make sure you ask for and obtain written substantiation for any income projections or income or profit claims. If the Franchiser does not have the required substantiation or refuses to provide it to you, consider its claims to be suspect.

Avoid High Pressure Sales Tactics

You may be told that the Franchiser's offering is limited, that there is only one territory left or that this is a one-time reduced franchise sales price. Do not feel pressured to make any commitment. Legitimate Franchisers expect you to comparison shop and to investigate their offering. A good deal today should be available tomorrow.

Study the Franchiser's Offering

Do not sign any contract or make any payment until you have the opportunity to investigate the Franchiser's offering thoroughly. As will be explained further in the next section, the FTC's Franchise Rule requires the Franchiser to provide you with a disclosure document containing important information about the franchise system. Study the disclosure document. Take time to speak with current and former franchisees about their experiences. Because investing in a franchise can entail a significant investment, you should have an attorney review the disclosure document and franchise contract and have an accountant review the company's financial disclosures.

Investigate Franchise Offerings

Before investing in any franchise system, be sure to get a copy of the Franchiser's disclosure document. Sometimes this document is called a Franchise Offering Circular. Under the FTC's Franchise Rule, you must receive the document at least 10 business days before you are asked to sign any contract or pay any money to the Franchiser. You should read the entire disclosure document. Make sure you understand all of the provisions. The following sections will help you to understand key provisions of typical disclosure documents and will help you ask questions about the disclosures. Get clarification of or answers to your concerns before you invest.

Business Background

The disclosure document identifies the executives of the franchise system and describes their prior experience. Consider not only their general business background but their experience in managing a franchise system. Also consider how long they have been with the company. Investing with an inexperienced Franchiser may be riskier than investing with an experienced one.

Litigation History

The disclosure document helps you assess the background of the Franchiser and its executives by requiring the disclosure of prior litigation. The disclosure document tells you if the Franchiser or any of its executive officers has been convicted of felonies involving, for example, fraud or if there have been any federal injunctions involving similar misconduct. It also will tell you if the Franchiser or any of its executives has been held liable or settled a civil action involving the franchise relationship. A number of claims against the Franchiser may indicate that it has not performed according to its agreements or, at the very least, that franchisees have been dissatisfied with the Franchiser's performance. Be aware that some Franchisers may try to conceal an executive's litigation history by removing the individual's name from their disclosure documents.

Bankruptcy

The disclosure document tells you if the Franchiser or any of its executives has recently been involved in a bankruptcy. This will help you to assess the Franchiser's financial stability and general business acumen and whether the company is financially capable of delivering promised support services.

Costs

The disclosure document tells you the costs involved with starting one of the company's franchises. It will describe any initial deposit or franchise fee, which may be nonrefundable, and costs for initial inventory, signs, equipment, leases or rentals. Be aware that there may be other undisclosed costs. The following checklist will help you ask about potential costs to you as a franchisee, including:

- continuing royalty payments
- advertising payments, both to local and national advertising funds
- grand opening or other initial business promotions
- business or operating licenses
- product or service supply costs
- real estate and leasehold improvements
- discretionary equipment such as a computer system or business alarm system
- training
- legal fees
- financial and accounting advice
- insurance
- compliance with local ordinances such as zoning, waste removal, and fire and other safety codes
- health insurance
- employee salaries and benefits

It may take several months or longer to get your business started. Consider in your total cost estimate the operating expenses for the first year and personal living expenses for up to 2 years. Compare your estimates with what other franchisees have paid and with competing franchise systems. Perhaps you can get a better deal with another Franchiser. An accountant can help you evaluate this information.

Restrictions

Your Franchiser may restrict how you operate your outlet. The disclosure document tells you if the Franchiser limits:

- the supplier from whom you may purchase goods;
- the goods or services you may offer for sale;
- the customers to whom you can offer goods or services; and
- the territory in which you can sell goods or services.

Understand that restrictions such as these may significantly limit your ability to exercise your own business judgment in operating your outlet.

Terminations

The disclosure document tells you the conditions under which the Franchiser may terminate your franchise and your obligations to the Franchiser after termination. It also tells you the conditions under which you can renew, sell or assign your franchise to other parties.

Training and Other Assistance

The disclosure document will explain the Franchiser's training and assistance program. Make sure you understand the level of training offered. The following checklist will help you ask the right questions.

- How many employees are eligible for training?
- Can new employees receive training, and if so, is there any additional cost?
- How long are the training sessions?
- How much time is spent on technical, business management and marketing training?
- Who teaches the training courses and what are their qualifications?
- What type of ongoing training does the company offer and at what cost?
- Whom can you speak to if problems arise?
- How many support personnel are assigned to your area?
- How many franchisees will the support personnel service?
- Will someone be available to come to your franchised outlet to provide more individual assistance?

The level of training you need depends on your own business experience and knowledge of the Franchiser's goods and services. Keep in mind that a primary reason for investing in the franchise as opposed to starting your own business is training and assistance. If you have doubts that the training might be insufficient to handle day-to-day business operations, consider another franchise opportunity more suited to your background.

Advertising

You often must contribute a percentage of your income to an advertising fund even if you disagree with how these funds are used. The disclosure document provides information on advertising costs. The following checklist will help you assess whether the Franchiser's advertising will benefit you.

- How much of the advertising fund is spent on administrative costs?
- Are there other expenses paid from the advertising fund?
- Do franchisees have any control over how the advertising dollars are spent?
- What advertising promotions has the company already engaged in?

- What advertising developments are expected in the near future?

- How much of the fund is spent on national advertising?

- How much of the fund is spent on advertising in your area?

- How much of the fund is spent on selling more franchises?

- Do all franchisees contribute equally to the advertising fund?

- Do you need the Franchiser's consent to conduct your own advertising?

- Are there rebates or advertising contribution discounts if you conduct your own advertising?

- Does the Franchiser receive any commissions or rebates when it places advertisements? Do franchisees benefit from such commissions or rebates, or does the Franchiser profit from them?

Current and Former Franchisees

The disclosure document provides important information about current and former franchisees. Determine how many franchises are currently operating. A large number of franchisees in your area may mean increased competition. Pay attention to the number of terminated franchisees. A large number of terminated, canceled or nonrenewed franchises may indicate problems. Be aware that some companies may try to conceal the number of failed franchisees by repurchasing failed outlets and then listing them as company-owned outlets.

If you buy an existing outlet, ask the Franchiser how many owners operated that outlet and over what period of time. A number of different owners over a short period of time may indicate that the location is not a profitable one or that the Franchiser has not supported that outlet with promised services.

The disclosure document gives you the names and addresses of current franchisees and franchisees that have left the system within the past year. Speaking with current or former franchisees is probably the most reliable way to verify the Franchiser's claims. Visit or phone as many of the current and former franchisees as possible. Ask them about their experiences. See for yourself the volume and type of business being done.

The following checklist will help you ask current and former franchisees questions.

- How long has the franchisee operated the franchise?

- Where is the franchise located?

- What was their total investment?

- Were there any hidden or unexpected costs?

- How long did it take them to cover operating costs and earn a reasonable income?

- Are they satisfied with the cost, delivery and quality of the goods or services sold?

- What were their backgrounds prior to becoming franchisees?

- Was the Franchiser's training adequate?

- What ongoing assistance does the Franchiser provide?

- Are they satisfied with the Franchiser's advertising program?

- Does the Franchiser fulfill its contractual obligations?

- Would the franchisee invest in another outlet?

- Would the franchisee recommend the investment to someone with your goals, income requirement and background?

Be aware that some Franchisers may give you a separate reference list of selected franchisees to contact. Be careful. Those on the list may be individuals who are paid by the Franchiser to give a good opinion of the company.

Earnings Potential

You may want to know how much money you can make if you invest in a particular franchise system. Be careful. Earnings projections can be misleading. Insist upon written substantiation for any earnings projections or suggestions about your potential income or sales.

Franchisers are not required to make earnings claims, but if they do, the FTC's Franchise Rule requires Franchisers to have a reasonable basis for these claims and to provide you with a document that substantiates them. This substantiation includes the basis and assumptions upon which these claims are made. Make sure you get and review the earnings claims document. Consider the following in reviewing any earnings claims.

Sample Size

A Franchiser may claim that franchisees in its system earned, for example, $50,000 last year. This claim may be deceptive, however, if only a few franchisees earned that income, and it does not represent the typical earnings of franchisees. Ask how many franchisees were included in the number.

Average Incomes

A Franchiser may claim that the franchisees in its system earn an average income of, for example, $75,000 a year. Average figures like this tell you very little about how each individual franchisee performs. Remember, a few very successful franchisees can inflate the average. An average figure may make the overall franchise system look more successful than it actually is.

Gross Sales

Some Franchisers provide figures for the gross sales revenues of their franchisees. These figures, however, do not tell you anything about the franchisees' actual costs or profits. An outlet with high gross sales revenue on paper actually may be losing money because of high overhead, rent and other expenses.

Net Profits

Franchisers often do not have data on net profits of their franchisees. If you do receive net profit statements, ask whether they provide information about company-owned outlets. Company-owned outlets might have lower costs because they can buy equipment, inventory and other items in larger quantities or may own rather than lease their property.

Geographic Relevance

Earnings may vary in different parts of the country. An ice cream store franchise in a southern state, such as Florida, may expect to earn more income than a similar franchise in a northern state, such as Minnesota. If you hear that a franchisee earned a particular income, ask where that outlet is located.

Franchisees' Backgrounds

Keep in mind that franchisees have varying levels of skills and educational backgrounds. Franchisees with advanced technical or business backgrounds can succeed in instances where more typical franchisees cannot. The success of some franchisees is no guarantee that you will be equally successful.

Financial History

The disclosure document provides you with important information about the company's financial status, including audited financial statements. Be aware that investing in a financially unstable franchiser is a significant risk; the company may go out of business or into bankruptcy after you have invested your money.

Hire a lawyer or an accountant to review the franchiser's financial statements. Do not attempt to extract this important information from the disclosure document unless you have considerable background in these matters. Your lawyer or accountant can help you understand the following:

- Does the Franchiser have steady growth?
- Does the Franchiser have a growth plan?
- Does the Franchiser make most of its income from the sale of franchises or from continuing royalties?
- Does the Franchiser devote sufficient funds to supporting its franchise system?

Additional Sources of Information

Before you invest in a franchise system, investigate the Franchiser thoroughly. In addition to reading the company's disclosure document and speaking with current and former franchisees, you should speak with the following individuals and institutions.

Lawyer and Accountant

Investing in a franchise is costly. An accountant can help you understand the company's financial statements, develop a business plan, and assess any earnings projections and the assumptions upon which they are based. An accountant can help you pick a franchise system that is best suited to your investment resources and your goals. If you are franchising a business with a partner remember to write up a partnership agreement.

Banks and Other Financial Institutions

These organizations may provide an unbiased view of the franchise opportunity you are considering. Your banker should be able to get a Dun & Bradstreet (D&B) credit report or similar reports on the Franchiser.

Better Business Bureau

Check with the local Better Business Bureau in the cities where the Franchiser has its headquarters. Ask if any consumers have complained about the company's products, services or personnel.

Government Departments

Several states regulate the sale of franchises. Check with your state division of securities or office of the attorney general for more information about your rights as a franchise owner in your state.

Federal Trade Commission

The FTC publishes other information that may be of interest to you, including business guides like "Getting Business Credit" and "Buying by Phone."

Frequently Asked Questions

The five most frequently asked questions about franchise and business opportunities are:

1. Where can I get a company's presale disclosure?

2. How can I find out about complaints against a company?

3. How can I file a complaint against a company?

4. Where can I get the forms for drafting an offering circular?

5. How can I find a lawyer who specializes in franchising?

Obtaining a Company's Presale Disclosure

The FTC does not require filings of franchise and business opportunity disclosure statements or offering circulars. For this reason, they are unable to provide copies of them. There are 13 states that do keep franchise offering circulars on file and 23 states that require business opportunity disclosure filings. Most states are not able to provide copies of these disclosures, but usually they will let you visit and review or copy the documents by appointment.

A few private companies may make available franchise disclosure documents filed in one or more states for a fee. These companies, which are neither supported nor endorsed by the FTC, include:

FRANdata Corp.	**FranchiseHelp, Inc.**
1.202.336.7632	1.914.347.6735
www.frandata.com	www.franchisehelp.com

Researching Complaints against a Company

No federal or state agency or private organization can tell you whether or not a company is legitimate or operates in good faith. They can only report on whether they have received consumer complaints about a company. Operators of fly-by-night franchise and business opportunity scams know this and may change the name and location of their company every 6 to 12 months so that they never have a record of consumer complaints.

There is no substitution for checking the track record of a Franchiser or business opportunity seller by talking to at least 10 prior purchasers in person. That is why the Franchise Rule requires companies to include in their disclosures a list of the names, addresses and telephone numbers of at least 10 prior purchasers who are geographically closest to you.

If you want information about consumer complaints, the FTC asks that your request be in writing. They need to check whether complaints have been received not only in Washington but also in one of their 10 regional offices. You can address your request to:

Freedom of Information Act Request

Office of General Counsel

Federal Trade Commission

600 Pennsylvania Ave. N.W.

Washington, D.C. 20580

Identify your letter as an FOIA Request and include:

• your name, address and daytime phone number; and

• the name and address of the company you are checking on.

In most cases, there are no fees for searching, document review or copying for members of the general public. It is a good idea, however, to state the maximum amount you are willing to pay, in the unusual event that any applicable fees for these services will cost more than the limit you set.

Filing a Complaint against a Company

The FTC cannot guarantee that they will be able to help in every case because the commission lacks the resources to investigate every individual complaint it receives. For this reason, they urge that you also consider talking with a private attorney about the feasibility of bringing a private lawsuit or taking other individual or group action that may help resolve the problem.

The FTC encourages you to send your complaint because consumer complaints give them important information. They help identify companies and practices that affect a broad segment of the public and are useful for law enforcement purposes.

They ask that all complaints be in writing, but no special form is required. Write a short one- or two-page letter telling what you think is misleading or deceptive in the company's promotional materials, disclosure statement or offering circular. If you want your letter kept confidential, include the words Privileged and Confidential on the top of each page.

Be sure your letter includes your name, address and a daytime telephone number where you can be reached. It will help if you can provide the names and telephone numbers of other purchasers who have experienced the same problems and if you can send copies of any written claims in promotional materials or elsewhere that you believe are false. Be sure to send copies, not originals, of any documents you think are important.

Address your complaints to:

Franchise and Business Opportunity Complaint

Federal Trade Commission—Room 238

Washington, D.C. 20580

Drafting an Offering Circular

The Franchise Rule provides its own disclosure format, which is published in the Code of Federal Regulations, Volume 16, Section 436 (16 CFR § 436). The FTC also permits the use of an alternative disclosure format called the Uniform Franchise Offering Circular (UFOC) issued by the North American Securities Administrators Association for Franchise Rule compliance. In order to comply with the Franchise Rule, Franchisers must follow the guidelines for preparing UFOC disclosures. A copy can be obtained from:

North American Securities Administrators Association, Inc.

750 First Street, N.E.

Suite 1140

Washington, D.C. 20002

1.202.737.0900

The current guidelines are also reprinted in the "Business Franchise Guide," which is available in many law libraries.

Locating a Lawyer Who Specializes in Franchising

You can start by checking with your state bar association. Many state bar associations allow member lawyers to identify the areas of practice in which they specialize, and franchise or distribution law is a recognized specialty in an increasing number of states.

The American Bar Association also publishes a membership directory of the "Forum Committee on Franchising". The directory, which is organized by state and city, lists the names, addresses and telephone numbers of attorneys who are members of the Forum Committee. To obtain a copy of the directory, an individual must be a member; it is not for sale to the public. Individuals may contact the ABA leadership for referrals or may be faxed a partial listing. Please visit www.abanet.org/forums/franchising for more information.

American Bar Association Service Center

321 North Clark Street

Chicago, IL 60610

1.312.988.5522

Pulling It All Together

Here are the components of a typical franchise system. Consider each carefully.

The Cost

What fees are involved?

Controls

What restrictions or controls are placed on franchisees?

- site approval   • restrictions on method of operation

- design or appearance standards   • restrictions of sales area

- restrictions on goods and services offered for sale

Your Investment

Before selecting a franchise system, inquire about:

- How much money do you have to invest?

- How much money can you afford to lose?

- Will you purchase the franchise by yourself or with partners?

- Will you need financing, and if so, where can you obtain it?

- Do you have a favorable credit rating?

- Do you have savings or additional income to live on while starting your franchise?

Your Abilities

- Does the franchise require technical experience or relevant education, such as auto repair, home and office decorating or tax preparation?

- What skills do you have? Do you have computer, bookkeeping or other technical skills?

- What specialized knowledge or talents can you bring to a business?

- Have you ever owned or managed a business?

Your Goals

- What are your goals?
- Do you require a specific level of annual income?
- Are you interested in pursuing a particular field?
- Are you interested in retail sales or performing a service?
- How many hours are you willing to work?
- Do you want to operate the business yourself or hire a manager?
- Will franchise ownership be your primary source of income or will it supplement your current income?
- Would you be happy operating the business for the next 20 years?
- Would you like to own several outlets or only one?

The Franchise

- What is the demand for the products or services, likely competition, the Franchiser's background and the level of support you will receive from the parent company?

Training and Support Services

- What training and ongoing support does the Franchiser provide?
- How does their training compare with the training for typical workers in the industry?
- Could you compete with others who have more formal training?
- What backgrounds do the current franchise owners have?
- Do they have prior technical backgrounds or special training that helps them succeed?
- Do you have a similar background?

Franchiser's Experience

- Carefully consider how long the Franchiser has managed a franchise system.
- Do you feel comfortable with the Franchiser's expertise?
- If Franchisers have little experience in managing a chain of franchises, their promises of guidance, training and other support may be unreliable.

Know How Much You Can Invest

- What amount do you feel comfortable investing or what is the maximum amount you can afford?

Know What Type of Business Is Right for You

> • Have you considered working in that industry before?
>
> • Can you see yourself engaged in that line of work for the next 20 years?
>
> • Do you have the necessary background or skills?

Comparison Shop

> • How long has the Franchiser been in business?
>
> • How many franchised outlets currently exist? Where are they located?
>
> • How much is the initial franchise fee and any additional startup costs? Are there any continuing royalty payments? How much are they?
>
> • What management, technical and ongoing assistance does the Franchiser offer?
>
> • What controls does the Franchiser impose?

Get Substantiation for Any Earnings Representations

Ask for and obtain written substantiation for any income projections or income or profit claims.

Litigation History

Bankruptcy

Have any of the company's executives recently been involved in a bankruptcy?

Costs

The following checklist items will help you determine potential costs:

> • continuing royalty payments
>
> • advertising payments, both to local and national advertising funds
>
> • grand opening or other initial business promotions
>
> • business or operating licenses
>
> • product or service supply costs
>
> • real estate and leasehold improvements
>
> • discretionary equipment such as a computer system or business alarm system
>
> • training
>
> • legal fees
>
> • financial and accounting advice
>
> • insurance
>
> • compliance with local ordinances such as zoning, waste removal, and fire and other safety codes
>
> • health insurance
>
> • employee salaries and benefits

Restrictions

Does the Franchiser limit:

> • the supplier from whom you may purchase goods;
> • the goods or services you may offer for sale;
> • the customers to whom you can offer goods or services; and
> • the territory in which you can sell goods or services?

Terminations

What are the conditions under which you can renew, sell or assign your franchise to other parties?

Training and Other Assistance

Ask the right questions:

> • How many employees are eligible for training?
> • Can new employees receive training, and if so, is there any additional cost?
> • How long are the training sessions?
> • How much time is spent on technical, business management and marketing training?
> • Who teaches the training courses and what are their qualifications?
> • What type of ongoing training does the company offer and at what cost?
> • Whom can you speak to if problems arise?
> • How many support personnel are assigned to your area?
> • How many franchisees will the support personnel service?
> • Will someone be available to come to your franchised outlet to provide more individual assistance?

Advertising

Assess whether the Franchiser's advertising will benefit you.

- How much of the advertising fund is spent on administrative costs?
- Are there other expenses paid from the advertising fund?
- Do franchisees have any control over how the advertising dollars are spent?
- What advertising promotions has the company already engaged in?
- What advertising developments are expected in the near future?
- How much of the fund is spent on national advertising?
- How much of the fund is spent on advertising in your area?
- How much of the fund is spent on selling more franchises?
- Do all franchisees contribute equally to the advertising fund?
- Do you need the Franchiser's consent to conduct your own advertising?
- Are there rebates or advertising contribution discounts if you conduct your own advertising?
- Does the Franchiser receive any commissions or rebates when it places advertisements? Do franchisees benefit from such commissions or rebates, or does the Franchiser profit from them?

Current and Former Franchisees

> • How many franchises are currently operating?
> • What is the number of terminated franchisees?

Ask current and former franchisees questions such as:

> • How long has the franchisee operated the franchise?
> • Where is the franchise located?
> • What was their total investment?
> • Were there any hidden or unexpected costs?
> • How long did it take them to cover operating costs and earn a reasonable income?
> • Are they satisfied with the cost, delivery and quality of the goods or services sold?
> • What were their backgrounds prior to becoming franchisees?
> • Was the Franchiser's training adequate?
> • What ongoing assistance does the Franchiser provide?
> • Are they satisfied with the Franchiser's advertising program?
> • Does the Franchiser fulfill its contractual obligations?
> • Would the franchisee invest in another outlet?
> • Would the franchisee recommend the investment to someone with your goals, income requirement and background?

Earnings Potential

Consider the following in reviewing any earnings claims:

> • sample size   • average incomes
> • gross sales   • net profits
> • geographic relevance • franchisees' backgrounds

Financial History

> • Does the Franchiser have steady growth?
> • Does the Franchiser have a growth plan?
> • Does the Franchiser make most of its income from the sale of franchises or from continuing royalties?
> • Does the Franchiser devote sufficient funds to supporting its franchise system?
> • How can I find out about complaints against a company?
> • How can I file a complaint against a company?
> • Where can I get the forms for drafting an offering circular?
> • How can I find a lawyer who specializes in franchising?

18 Sample Business Plans

Overview

Reading about how to create a business plan is important, but writing it is something different. Enclosed on the accompanying CD, you will find three sample business plans to help jump-start your new business. They include:

- services company business plan—Hometown Realty Inc.
- not-for-profit organization business plan—New England Motor Sports Business
- retail operations business plan—The Royal Bean

An Important Note

These sample business plans are intended for use as examples only. All information included in each plan is fictitious. Any resemblance to actual companies is purely coincidental and is not intended to compete with or divulge proprietary ideas, company structure or financial status of any company.

Section Seven

Supporting Documents

Overview

Your business plan document should include any supporting documents that will help state and support your idea. Include in the back of the plan–in an appendix format–any supporting documentation you may have. Make a list of all the items you can think of and gather them as you are working on your plan. Position them in the plan in a logical order and number or name them for easy identification.

Supporting documentation may include:

The Household Census Survey

The Census Bureau survey collects information about education, employment, income and housing—information your community uses to plan and fund programs. The American Community Survey (ACS) is a new nationwide survey designed to provide communities with a fresh look at how they are changing. It is intended to eliminate the need for the long form in the 2010 census. The new ACS just began going out to 250,000 households across the country every month. This rolling survey will give large cities a detailed demographic picture of their populations every year rather than every 10 years. Eventually, smaller communities will have similar data. To a community that is growing rapidly, it provides a yearly growth snapshot. Include any consumer or business demographic information that will support your plan.

"How much support material/documentation is necessary? The more money you are asking others to risk, the more hard data you need to include in the appendix. The more research, more statistics, more articles and interviews you provide, the less subjective your business will be. The more money you are asking from others, the thicker the documentation should be."

Sara Shifrin
Director of Entrepreneur Training
Women's Business Development Center
Chicago, IL

The ACS will collect information from U.S. households similar to what was collected on the 2000 census long form, such as income, commute time to work, home value, veteran status and other important data. As with the official U.S. census, information about individuals will remain confidential.

Data Profile Includes:

- **Demographic**—sex and age, race, relationship, household by type
- **Social**—education, marital status, fertility, grandparents, etc.
- **Economic**—income, employment, occupation, commuting to work, etc.
- **Housing**—occupancy and structure, housing value and costs, utilities, etc.
- **Narrative**—text profile with graphs for easy analysis

The data includes information about age, social characteristics, economic characteristics and housing characteristics.

Fact sheets for specific geographic areas are available at the U.S. Census Bureau Web site http://factfinder.census.gov/home/saff/main.html?_lang=en&_ts= and look like this:

American Community Survey Statistics

General Characteristics	Estimate	Percent	U.S.
Total population	2,722,562	100.0	100.0%
Male	1,322,402	48.6	48.9%
Female	1,400,160	51.4	51.1%
Median age (years)	32.3	(X)	36.0%
Under 5 years	217,615	8.0	7.0%
18 years and over	2,008,771	73.8	74.3%
65 years and over	279,189	10.3	12.0%
One race total	2,685,962	98.7	98.1%
White	1,276,492	46.9	76.1%
Black or African American	983,655	36.1	12.1%
American Indian and Alaska Native	5,580	0.2	0.8%
Asian	119,455	4.4	4.1%
Native Hawaiian and Other Pacific Islander	2,382	0.1	0.1%
Some other race	298,398	11.0	4.8%
Two or more races	36,600	1.3	1.9%
Hispanic or Latino (of any race)	746,115	27.4	13.8%
Average household size	2.7	(X)	2.6
Average family size	3.61	(X)	3.2
Total housing units	1,146,060	100.0	100.0%
Occupied housing units	1,009,012	88.0	89.7%
Owner-occupied housing units	478,384	47.4	66.8%
Renter-occupied housing units	530,628	52.6	33.2%
Vacant housing units	137,048	12.0	10.3%

Social Characteristics	Estimate	Percent	U.S.
Population 25 years or over	1,734,388	100.0	---
High school graduate or higher	(X)	77.4	83.6%
Bachelor's degree or higher	(X)	28.1	26.5%
Civilian veterans (civilian population 18 years and over)	118,919	5.9	11.4%
Disability status (population 21 to 64 years)	161,700	9.9	12.0%
Foreign born	586,859	21.6	11.8%
Male, now married (population 15 years and over)	429,555	42.3	56.6%
Female, now married (population 15 years and over)	400,510	36.5	51.6%
Speak a language other than English at home (for the population 5 years and over)	883,208	35.3	18.4%
Economic Characteristics	**Estimate**	**Percent**	**U.S.**
In labor force (population 16 years and over)	1,338,955	64.4	66.0%
Mean travel time to work in minutes (population 16 years and over)	33.2	(X)	24.3
Median household income (dollars)	40,879	(X)	43564.0%
Median family income (dollars)	43,848	(X)	52273.0%
Per capita income (dollars)	21,773	(X)	23110.0%
Families below poverty level	98,358	16.6	9.8%
Individuals below poverty level	523,772	19.3	12.7%
Housing Characteristics	**Estimate**	**Percent**	**U.S.**
Singe-family owner-occupied homes	269,457	100.0	---
Median value (dollars)	176,675	(X)	147,275
Median of selected monthly owner costs	(X)	(X)	---
With a mortgage	1,399	(X)	1,204
Not mortgaged	428	(X)	333

(x) Not applicable

Source: U.S. Census Bureau, 2003 American Community Survey

Functional Resumes

Include a resume for each partner, or if you are a sole proprietorship, your own. If you are a corporation, include resumes of all officers. Each resume should contain specific information and should be no longer than one page. Information to include:

Work history

Include the name and address of each place of employment along with dates employed. Start with the most recent employment and work backwards. Include duties, responsibilities and related accomplishments.

Educational background

List schools attended, dates attended, degrees earned and your fields of concentration or studies. Include any additional skills or courses completed and any certifications earned.

Professional Affiliations and Honors

List any active affiliations with professional organizations related to your industry. Include any professional recognitions or awards received.

Special Skills

List any skills that single you out as an asset to the organization, such as gets along well with others, adept at multitasking and organized.

Sample Floor Plan

If you are leasing space, include a copy of the office or building floor plan. Show how the space will be utilized, where employees will be positioned and potential adjustments as the company grows. Include commentary describing parking, location, benefits of the area and why the particular site was chosen. Also include how other space in the same area compares to the site you selected.

Sample Partnership Agreement

Every good partnership begins with an ironclad agreement outlining responsibilities and distribution of money. The agreement should include the following information:

Length of Partnership

Usually a partnership agreement is in perpetuity unless a partner requests to be bought out or is willing to give up his or her share of the business. There are specific reasons when a partnership may dissolve—for example, if the business reaches a certain size or when profits become large enough to repay a partner's initial investment.

Partner Contributions of Time or Money

The amount of time or money partners contribute will rarely be the same. One partner may contribute more money than time, another may contribute more time than money. A good agreement will take into account the imbalance and will spell out ways to balance out the inequities.

Business Decisions

In the event that the partners may not agree on a weighty decision, the agreement will include provisions to encourage a decision. Disagreements have a tendency to stop all production or forward momentum gained. Including a provision to force decision making progress will keep the business healthy.

Sharing of Profits and Losses

Often profit-sharing and loss-sharing go hand in hand and are divided equally between partners. However, occasionally one partner may absorb a greater loss or enjoy a greater profit than the other partners. When this occurs, the unequal distribution should be spelled out in advance—the agreement should provide parameters that may include an increase of responsibility, new investments or adjusted workloads as compensation.

Owner's Financial Statement

This is a statement of the owner's personal assets and liabilities and may be formatted like a balance sheet. It is also a statement of annual income and expenditure. If you are a new business, the owner's financial statement will be included as a part of any financial documentation you provide in the finance section of the plan. This personal financial statement may include the following information:

- assets including cash, account receivables, stocks and bonds, life insurance cash value, automobile makes and years, real estate holdings and other assets
- liabilities including outstanding payments due, any notes due, tax payments, outstanding balances on contracts, real estate debt and miscellaneous liabilities
- annual income from salary, dividends, interest, securities, rental units, etc.
- annual expenditures including real estate payments, rent, income taxes, insurance premiums and any other installment payments due
- your net income derived from subtracting total expenditures from total income

Credit Reports

Include a copy of any credit rating you may have—both business and personal. Personal credit reports may be obtained upon request from credit bureaus, such as TRW and Experian, banks and other companies that you have dealt with on a credit basis. It is important that you review your credit history at least twice a year to correct any errors that may pop up on your report. It is best to correct them quickly to maintain a clean credit history. A good report is rewarded with lower interest rates and more favorable terms. A bad or spotty credit report will cost you more money in the long run.

Copies of Leases

Include copies of all lease agreements that are currently in force between your company and a leasing agent. Lease agreements may include equipment, automobiles, furniture, etc. Lease information helps support any financial information that you have provided in your financial statements.

Letters of Reference

Letters of reference present you to investors as a reputable businessperson and, in the recommending person's opinion, a good business risk. There are two types of references:

Business Reference

These letters are generally written by a business associate, supplier or customer.

Personal Reference

This type of letter is usually written by a nonbusiness associate who is able to vouch for your business acumen based on his or her personal association with you. Personal references generally are not written by close friends or relatives.

Contracts

Include copies of all contracts—those that are still in force and those that have been completed. Examples of contracts to include are:

- current loan contracts
- papers on previous business loans
- purchase agreements on large and small equipment
- vehicle or automobile purchase agreements—for personal and company vehicles
- service contracts—be sure to include costs, length of agreement and the equipment covered
- maintenance agreements—include costs, length of agreement and equipment covered, a short narrative of how the maintenance agreement saves you time and money and why you decided to purchase the agreement
- miscellaneous agreements—any other agreements that affect monthly payments or profit margins

Legal Documents

Include copies of all legal documents associated with your business, including:

- articles of incorporation
- life insurance policies of partners, copies of premiums and agreements
- partnership agreements
- doing business as (DBA) filings and agreements with each state/county
- business licenses
- filings for any copyrights, trademarks, service marks and patents
- trade agreements between companies and countries
- licensing agreements—domestic and international
- property and vehicle titles

Miscellaneous Documents

Include any other types of documentation that will support your business idea and studies. If you have community data available—economic studies, forecasts, crime statistics, planned community renovations, area upgrades or proposed building—include this information in your plan. Provide information about the area surrounding your chosen location. Include demographic studies to support how the location was selected, surrounding businesses, foot traffic, etc.

The more supporting materials you can provide the stronger your business plan will become.

Pulling It All Together

Check off all supporting documentation included in your plan:

	Household census survey
	Resumes of key partners and employees
	Floor plan
	Partnership agreement
	Personal financial report of owner and partners
	Credit report of owner or partners
	Copy of lease
	Letters of reference
	Copies of all equipment, loan and service contracts
	Articles of incorporation
	Life insurance policies
	Trademark, copyright, service mark and patent agreements
	Trade agreements between companies
	Licensing agreements
	Property and vehicle titles
	Miscellaneous documents

20 U.S. Tax Information

Overview

The IRS never rests. They have created an increasingly complex and ever-changing labyrinth of tax forms for even the smallest mom and pop operations. Tax time is a lot less hectic when your books are accurate, organized and up-to-date year-round. Completing IRS forms can be largely a matter of plugging in figures from your profit and loss statement and income and expense ledgers. It may pay to hire an accountant to make sure you not only comply with legal requirements but also maximize your deductions. This chapter will help you better plan for tax time.

> **Hint**
>
> If you are a sole proprietor with no employees, pay no excise tax and did not inherit the business, you may be able to use your Social Security number for tax purposes. All other cases require a federal Employer Identification Number (EIN).

Separating a Business from a Hobby

It is generally accepted that people prefer to make a living doing something they like. A hobby is an activity for which you do not expect to make a profit. If you do not carry on your business or investment activity to make a profit, there is a limit on the deductions you can take.

You must include on your return income from an activity from which you do not expect to make a profit. An example of this type of activity is a hobby or a farm that you operate mostly for recreation and pleasure. You cannot use a loss from the activity to offset other income. Activities you do as a hobby or mainly for sport or recreation come under this limit. So does an investment activity intended only to produce tax losses for the investors.

The limit on not-for-profit losses applies to individuals, partnerships, estates, trusts and S corporations. For additional information on these entities, refer to business structures. It does not apply to corporations other than S corporations.

In determining whether you are carrying on an activity for profit, all the factors are taken into account. No one factor is decisive. Among the factors to consider are whether:

- you carry on the activity in a businesslike manner;
- the time and effort you put into the activity indicate that you intend to make it profitable;
- you depend on income from the activity for your livelihood;
- your losses are due to circumstances beyond your control or are normal in the startup phase of your type of business;
- you change your methods of operation in an attempt to improve profitability;
- you or your advisors have the knowledge needed to carry on the activity as a successful business;
- you were successful in making a profit in similar activities in the past;
- the activity makes a profit in some years and the amount of profit it makes; and
- you can expect to make a future profit from the appreciation of the assets used in the activity.

Tips for Managing Your Taxes

- **Get an accountant on day one.**
- **Make sure the accountant has experience in your industry or a business of your size.**
- **If you work with an accountant who is accustomed to working with a small company, they will remind you of the critical deadlines.**
- **Before you start, have an accountant come in and set up your software— create the books for how they will use them to keep your business afloat.**
- **Get set up on an electronic bookkeeping system.**
- **Seek out new technologies that will remind you of the taxes to pay.**
- **Employee taxes often trip up small-business owners.**
- **Set up virtual bookkeeping reminders.**

Kelly Mizeur
Finance Counselor
Women's Business Development Center
Chicago, IL

Calendar Year vs. Fiscal Year

When you apply for an (EIN), you will note that the IRS asks you to declare a fiscal year start and end. In some states, even the certificate of incorporation requires the fiscal year to be given. Of course, it is easiest to choose the calendar year as your corporation's fiscal year. However, if that is impossible, a second choice would be July 1 to June 30. In that case, for your first year of incorporation, you would have to file two sets of income tax forms: For the first half of the year, you would file an individual return as a sole proprietor using Schedule C and any other appropriate schedules. For the second half of the year, you would file a corporate return—Form 1120, or Form 1120S if you make a Subchapter S election— and an individual return, because you would then be an employee of your corporation.

Similarly, if you chose April 1 to October 1 as the beginning of your fiscal year, you would have to file the same two sets of tax returns. If you chose April 1, you would file as a sole proprietor for the first quarter–January 1 to March 31–and you would file corporate and individual returns for the last three quarters–April 1 to December 31. If you chose October 1, you would file as a sole proprietor for the first three quarters–January 1 to September 30–and corporate and individual returns for the last quarter–October 1 to December 31.

The advantage of a separate fiscal year is that it allows flexibility in tax planning. By having two tax years to work with, you and your accountant have more flexibility in tax planning. And the corporate and personal tax savings can be significant. You may want to choose a fiscal year on the advice of your accountant, who can determine the fiscal year most advantageous to you. If you choose the calendar year as your fiscal year, you will have fewer tax forms to file. However, there may be advantages to choosing a different fiscal year.

Tax Information from the IRS

Advice from an IRS agent is not always reliable. However, you can obtain surprisingly clear and helpful information from several IRS publications, including:

- Starting a Business and Keeping Records— Publication 583
- Tax Guide for Small Business—Publication 334
- Employer's Tax Guide—Circular E
- Tax Calendars—Publication 509
- Tax Withholding and Estimated Tax—Publication 505

Self-Employment Tax

Many people are not aware of the self-employment tax, also known as Self-Employment Contributions Act tax. According to 1997 figures, sole proprietorships, partners and active owners in LLCs must pay tax on business income if they earn more than $400 in a given year.

If you operate at a loss, you owe no income tax on the business. You can also apply this net operating loss to other taxable personal income or allow the credit to carry over to other years. If you are unable to generate a profit over several years, the IRS may rule your venture is a hobby and disallow any tax benefits.

Hint

It is advisable to earmark a portion of your income and financial assets for taxes—20 to 25 percent is a good start. Anything left over can be used as a capital investment fund or bonus. This is especially important for sole proprietors who have to pay self-employment tax, which makes up your share of Social Security and Medicare payments.

Employee and Payroll Taxes

If you hire employees, prepare to devote about 30 percent of your payroll to taxes and paperwork. You are responsible for withholding all of your full- or part-time employees' federal and state income tax, Social Security and Medicare taxes from paychecks, remitting them with your overall tax bill. You also must pay your portion of Social Security and Medicare benefit funds. On employee salaries up to $87,922, you are taxed 6.2 percent for Social Security and 1.45 percent for Medicare.

Payroll taxes–including withholding–are due quarterly on these dates:

- April 30 for wages paid January–March
- July 31 for April–June
- October 31 for July–September
- January 31 for October–December

If owed taxes exceed $500, the due date becomes the fifteenth day of the next month.

Independent Contractors

You may be able to save paperwork and expenses by hiring independent contractors. These workers are in business for themselves, pay their own taxes and insurance, use their own equipment and facilities, require little or no supervision and are typically paid per project. To avoid threat of tax fraud and liability charges, make sure the above factors apply and make these points clear to the workers. A written independent contractor's agreement is the best protection against potentially expensive or damaging misunderstandings. When hiring an independent contractor, be sure to record his or her full name, address and Social Security or EIN.

An employer does not generally have to withhold or pay any taxes on payments to independent contractors. The general rule is that an individual is an independent contractor if the person for whom the services are performed has the right to control or direct only the result of the work and not what will be done and how it will be done or the method of accomplishing the result.

People such as lawyers, contractors, subcontractors, public stenographers and auctioneers who follow an independent trade, business or profession in which they offer their services to the public are generally not employees. However, whether such people are employees or independent contractors depends on the facts in each case. The earnings of a person who is working as an independent contractor are subject to Self-Employment (SE) tax.

The employer, however, is responsible for asking all independent contractors to complete an FDIC Substitute Form W-9 Request for Taxpayer Identification Number and Certification. This form provides the independent contractor's correct taxpayer identification number to the company who in turn must report any income paid above $600 to an independent contractor.

A copy of the FDIC Substitute Form W-9 Request for Taxpayer Identification Number and Certification form may be found on the Web landing page www.socrates.com/books/business-plan.aspx.

Business Expenses

To qualify as a deduction from your taxable income, expenses must be business related, ordinary, necessary and reasonable. Keep accurate tabs on expenses by paying from your business account, entering expenses in the appropriate expense ledger category and keeping all receipts. Expenses must be recorded as what you actually paid out—not market value. Interest charges for purchases are not deductible. Barter economy is treated like any other business income based on fair market value.

Deducting startup costs may be complicated and may require the help of an accountant. Business-related startup expenses may be deducted in one of two ways: They may be capitalized at the time you quit or sell your business or amortized monthly over a 60-month period. (See next section, Depreciation.)

The IRS also frequently denies deductions until the business actually makes a sale, although tax courts contend that denial as long as they are conducting business. In either case, it is a good idea to put off as many expenses as possible until you are conducting business.

To be eligible for business deductions, your business must be an activity undertaken with the intent of making a profit. It is presumed that you meet this requirement if your business makes a profit in any 2 years of a 5-year period.

Once you are this far along, you can deduct business expenses such as supplies, subscriptions to professional journals and an allowance for the business use of your car or truck. You can also claim deductions for home-related business expenses such as utilities and in some cases, even a new paint job on your home. The IRS is going to treat the part of your home you use for business as though it were a separate piece of property. This means that you will have to keep good records and take care not to mix business and personal matters. No specific method of record-keeping is required, but your records must clearly justify any deductions you claim. Before making any tax deduction for your home office or any other home office expense, be sure to consult with your tax advisor.

Depreciation

Over time, business equipment ages, deteriorates or becomes obsolete. You can get back a portion of your cost for certain property by taking deductions for depreciation. Items you acquire before starting your operation may be depreciated based on their market value at the time you began using them for business. Major repairs and improvements may also be depreciated.

Generally, to depreciate your assets, the property must be used in your business or income-producing activity. You stop depreciating the property when you have recovered its cost or other basis or when you retire it from service, whichever comes first. The kind of property you own affects how you can claim a depreciation deduction. Property falls into two categories: tangible and intangible.

Tangible property is property that can be seen or touched, such as buildings, cars, machinery or equipment. If you own tangible property that you use for both personal and business purposes, you may take deductions based only on the business use portion of the property. Certain types of property can never be depreciated. For example, you cannot depreciate the cost of land, because it does not wear out or become obsolete. The cost of inventory does not qualify for the depreciation deduction either.

Intangible property is generally any property that cannot be seen or touched, such as copyrights, franchises or patents. Certain types of intangible property cannot be depreciated, but must be amortized instead. To see if you can claim depreciation deductions, view Form 4562, Depreciation and Amortization for instructions.

You may be able to deduct all or part of the cost of certain qualifying property used in your business in the year you placed it in service by claiming a Section 179 deduction—"Election to Expense Certain Business Assets." The advantage of claiming the Section 179 deduction is that you get to deduct more up front. Like depreciation deductions, you can claim the Section 179 deduction only when your property is ready to be used in your business or income-producing activity.

There are limitations. For example, if the cost of all qualifying property in 2004 is $400,000 or more, the maximum Section 179 deduction you can take is reduced by the amount over $400,000. When the cost of all qualifying property in 2004 exceeds $500,000, then no Section 179 deduction is allowed. The maximum Section 179 deduction for 2004 is $100,000. You cannot deduct costs in excess of your taxable income, which includes your trade and business income, plus your wages and salaries for the year. Use Form 4562 to make the election to claim a Section 179 deduction or carry-over.

If you decide taxable profits at year's end are too small to warrant immediate deduction, you may choose to write the costs according to depreciation of any or all items with a life of over 1 year. This means you deduct the cost of an item divided over several years. Length of depreciation ranges from 3 to 39 years depending on the type of goods.

The U.S. Tax System

During the tax year, all businesses must adhere to all reporting and payment schedules. Not all reporting dates are the same and are dependent on the type of legal structure you have selected for your business.

Each organization type has different reporting and filing dates. To locate filing dates, find the legal structure that best describes your organization to review your company's key filing dates.

Sole Proprietor Calendar Worksheet

January 15	Estimated tax filing	Form 1040ES
April 15	Estimated tax filing	Form 1040ES
June 15	Estimated tax filing	Form 1040ES
September 15	Estimated tax filing	Form 1040ES
January 31	Social Security (FICA) tax and income tax withholding	Forms 941, 941E, 942 and 943
April 30	Social Security (FICA) tax and income tax withholding	Forms 941, 941E, 942 and 943
July 31	Social Security (FICA) tax and income tax withholding	Forms 941, 941E, 942 and 943

October 31	Social Security (FICA) tax and income tax withholding	Forms 941, 941E, 942 and 943
January 31	Providing information on Social Security (FICA) tax and the withholding of income tax to employee	Form W-2
January 31	Federal Unemployment Tax (FUTA)	Form 940-EZ or 940
January 31	Federal Unemployment Tax (FUTA) (only if liability for unpaid taxes exceeds $100)	Form 8109 to make deposits
April 15	Federal Unemployment Tax (FUTA) (only if liability for unpaid taxes exceeds $100)	Form 8109 to make deposits
July 31	Federal Unemployment Tax (FUTA) (only if liability for unpaid taxes exceeds $100)	Form 8109 to make deposits
October 31	Federal Unemployment Tax (FUTA) (only if liability for unpaid taxes exceeds $100)	Form 8109 to make deposits
January 31	Statement returns to nonemployees and transactions with other or independent contractors	Form 1099 to individuals
February 28	Statement returns to nonemployees and transactions with other or independent contractors	Form 1099 to IRS
April 15	Income tax filing	Schedule C (Form 1040)
April 15	Self-employment tax filing	Schedule SE (Form 1040)

If your tax year is not January 1 through December 31:

Schedule C (Form 1040) is due on the fifteenth day of the fourth month after the end of your tax year.

Schedule SE is due the same day as income tax (Form 1040).

Estimated Tax (1040ES) is due on the fifteenth day of the fourth, sixth and ninth months of the tax year and the fifteenth day of the first month after the end of your tax year.

Partnership Calendar Worksheet

January 15	Estimated tax filing by individual who is a partner	Form 1040ES
April 15	Estimated tax filing by individual who is a partner	Form 1040ES
June 15	Estimated tax filing by individual who is a partner	Form 1040ES
September 15	Estimated tax filing by individual who is a partner	Form 1040ES
January 31	Social Security (FICA) tax and income tax withholding	Forms 941, 941E, 942 and 943
April 30	Social Security (FICA) tax and income tax withholding	Forms 941, 941E, 942 and 943
July 31	Social Security (FICA) tax and income tax withholding	Forms 941, 941E, 942 and 943
October 31	Social Security (FICA) tax and income tax withholding	Forms 941, 941E, 942 and 943
January 31	Providing information on Social Security (FICA) tax and the withholding of income tax to employee	Form W-2
January 31	Federal Unemployment Tax (FUTA)	Form 940-EZ or 940
January 31	Federal Unemployment Tax (FUTA) (only if liability for unpaid taxes exceeds $100)	Form 8109 to make deposits
April 15	Federal Unemployment Tax (FUTA) (only if liability for unpaid taxes exceeds $100)	Form 8109 to make deposits
July 31	Federal Unemployment Tax (FUTA) (only if liability for unpaid taxes exceeds $100)	Form 8109 to make deposits
October 31	Federal Unemployment Tax (FUTA) (only if liability for unpaid taxes exceeds $100)	Form 8109 to make deposits
January 31	Statement returns to nonemployees and transactions with other or independent contractors	Form 1099 to individuals
February 28	Statement returns to nonemployees and transactions with other or independent contractors	Form 1099 to IRS
February 28	Providing information on Social Security (FICA) tax and the withholding of income tax to employee	Forms W-2 and W-3 to SSA
April 15	Income tax filing	Schedule C (Form 1040)
April 15	Annual return of income	Form 1065
April 15	Self-employment tax filing (by individual who is a partner)	Schedule SE (Form 1040)

If your tax year is not January 1 through December 31:

Income tax is due on the fifteenth day of the fourth month after the end of your tax year.

Schedule SE is due the same day as income tax (Form 1040).

Estimated Tax (1040ES) is due on the fifteenth day of the fourth, sixth and ninth months of the tax year and the 15th day of the 1st month after the end of your tax year.

Discounts on Other Socrates Products

In addition to a variety of free forms and checklists, you will find special offers on a variety of Socrates products.

Visit www.socrates.com/books/business-plan.aspx for more information.

S Corporation Calendar Worksheet

January 15	Estimated tax filing (by individual S corporation shareholder)	Form 1040ES
April 15	Estimated tax filing (by individual S corporation shareholder)	Form 1040ES
June 15	Estimated tax filing (by individual S corporation shareholder)	Form 1040ES
September 15	Estimated tax filing (by individual S corporation shareholder)	Form 1040ES
January 31	Social Security (FICA) tax and income tax withholding	Forms 941, 941E, 942 and 943
April 30	Social Security (FICA) tax and income tax withholding	Forms 941, 941E, 942 and 943
July 31	Social Security (FICA) tax and income tax withholding	Forms 941, 941E, 942 and 943
October 31	Social Security (FICA) tax and income tax withholding	Forms 941, 941E, 942 and 943
January 31	Providing information on Social Security (FICA) tax and the withholding of income tax to employee	Form W-2
January 31	Federal Unemployment Tax (FUTA)	Form 940-EZ or 940
January 31	Federal Unemployment Tax (FUTA) (only if liability for unpaid taxes exceeds $100)	Form 8109 to make deposits
April 15	Federal Unemployment Tax (FUTA) (only if liability for unpaid taxes exceeds $100)	Form 8109 to make deposits
July 31	Federal Unemployment Tax (FUTA) (only if liability for unpaid taxes exceeds $100)	Form 8109 to make deposits
October 31	Federal Unemployment Tax (FUTA) (only if liability for unpaid taxes exceeds $100)	Form 8109 to make deposits
January 31	Statement returns to nonemployees and transactions with other or independent contractors	Form 1099 to individuals
February 28	Statement returns to nonemployees and transactions with other or independent contractors	Form 1099 to IRS
February 28	Providing information on Social Security (FICA) tax and the withholding of income tax to employee	Forms W-2 and W-3 to SSA
April 15	Income tax filing	Form 1120S
April 15	Income tax filing (individual S corporation shareholder)	Form 1040

If your tax year is not January 1 through December 31:

Income Tax (Form 1120 or 1120-A) is due on the fifteenth day of the third month after the end of your tax year.

Estimated Tax (1120-W) is due on the fifteenth day of the fourth, sixth, ninth and twelfth months of the tax year.

Corporation Calendar Worksheet

April 15	Estimated tax filing by individual who is a partner	Form 1120W
June 15	Estimated tax filing by individual who is a partner	Form 1120W
September 15	Estimated tax filing by individual who is a partner	Form 1120W
December 15	Estimated tax filing by individual who is a partner	Form 1120W
January 31	Social Security (FICA) tax and income tax withholding	Forms 941, 941E, 942 and 943
April 30	Social Security (FICA) tax and income tax withholding	Forms 941, 941E, 942 and 943
July 31	Social Security (FICA) tax and income tax withholding	Forms 941, 941E, 942 and 943
October 31	Social Security (FICA) tax and income tax withholding	Forms 941, 941E, 942 and 943
January 31	Providing information on Social Security (FICA) tax and the withholding of income tax to employee	Form W-2
January 31	Federal Unemployment Tax (FUTA)	Form 940-EZ or 940
January 31	Federal Unemployment Tax (FUTA) (only if liability for unpaid taxes exceeds $100)	Form 8109 to make deposits
April 15	Federal Unemployment Tax (FUTA) (only if liability for unpaid taxes exceeds $100)	Form 8109 to make deposits
July 31	Federal Unemployment Tax (FUTA) (only if liability for unpaid taxes exceeds $100)	Form 8109 to make deposits
October 31	Federal Unemployment Tax (FUTA) (only if liability for unpaid taxes exceeds $100)	Form 8109 to make deposits
January 31	Statement returns to nonemployees and transactions with other or independent contractors	Form 1099 to individuals
February 28	Statement returns to nonemployees and transactions with other or independent contractors	Form 1099 to IRS
March 15	Income tax filing	Form 1120 or 1120-A

If your tax year is not January 1 through December 31:

Income tax is due on the fifteenth day of the fourth month after the end of your tax year.

Schedule SE is due the same day as income tax (Form 1040).

Estimated Tax (1040ES) is due on the fifteenth day of the fourth, sixth and ninth months of the tax year and the fifteenth day of the first month after the end of your tax year.

Employment Taxes

Small-business owners often have great responsibilities while operating and managing a business. Before you become an employer and hire employees, you need a federal EIN.

If you have employees, you are responsible for several federal, state and local taxes. As an employer, you must withhold certain taxes from your employees' paychecks. Employment taxes include the following:

- Federal income tax withholding
- Social Security and Medicare taxes
- Federal Unemployment Tax Act (FUTA)
- Federal income taxes/Social Security and Medicare taxes

You generally must withhold federal income tax from your employees' wages. To figure how much to withhold from each wage payment, use the employee's Form W-4 and the methods described in Publication 15, Employer's Tax Guide and Publication 15-A, Employer's Supplemental Tax Guide.

Social Security and Medicare taxes pay for benefits that workers and families receive under the Federal Insurance Contributions Act. Social Security tax pays for benefits under the oldage, survivors and disability insurance part of FICA. Medicare tax pays for benefits under the hospital insurance part of FICA. You withhold part of these taxes from your employees' wages and you pay a matching amount yourself.

To report federal income taxes, Social Security and Medicare taxes use Form 941, Employer's Quarterly Federal Tax Return or Form 943, Employer's Annual Federal Tax Return for Agriculture Employees if you are a farmer who maintains employees.

Federal Unemployment Tax

The federal unemployment tax is part of the federal and state program under the Federal Unemployment Tax Act that pays unemployment compensation to workers who lose their jobs. You report and pay FUTA tax separately from Social Security and Medicare taxes and withheld income tax. You pay FUTA tax only from your own funds. Employees do not pay this tax or have it withheld from their pay. Report FUTA taxes on Form 940, Employer's Annual Federal Unemployment (FUTA) Tax Return, or if you qualify, you can use the simpler Form 940-EZ instead.

Depositing Taxes

In general, you must deposit income tax withheld and both the employer and employee Social Security and Medicare taxes (minus any advance EIC payments) by mailing or delivering a check, money order or cash to a financial institution that is an authorized depository for federal taxes. However, some taxpayers are required to deposit using the Electronic Federal Tax Deposit System. For additional information, call the IRS or visit www.irs.gov and go to the IRS Employment Taxes for Small Businesses page.

Independent Contractors vs. Employees

Before you can determine how to treat payments you make for services, you first must know the business relationship that exists between you and the person performing the services. The person performing the services may be:

- an independent contractor
- a common law employee
- a statutory employee
- a statutory nonemployee

In determining whether the person providing service is an employee or an independent contractor, all information that provides evidence of the degree of control and independence must be considered.

It is critical that you, the employer, correctly determine whether the individuals providing services are employees or independent contractors. Generally, you must withhold income taxes, withhold and pay Social Security and Medicare taxes, and pay unemployment tax on wages paid to an employee. You do not generally have to withhold or pay any taxes on payments to independent contractors.

Caution

If you incorrectly classify an employee as an independent contractor, you can be held liable for employment taxes for that worker, plus a penalty.

Determining Who Is an Independent Contractor

A general rule is that you, the payer, have the right to control or direct only the result of the work done by an independent contractor, and not the means and methods of accomplishing the result.

Example

Suzy Smith, a marketing consultant, submitted a job estimate to a company for marketing work at $40 per hour for 400 hours. She is to receive $1,600 every week for the next 10 weeks. This is not considered payment by the hour. Even if she works more or less than 400 hours to complete the work, Suzy will receive $16,000. She also performs additional marketing projects under contracts with other companies. Suzy is an independent contractor.

Reporting Payments Made to Independent Contractors

You may be required to file information returns to report certain types of payments made to independent contractors during the year. For example, you must file Form 1099-MISC, Miscellaneous Income, to report payments of $600 or more to persons not treated as employees—e.g., independent contractors—for services performed for your trade or business. For details about filing Form 1099 and for information about required electronic or magnetic media filing, refer to information returns.

What Is a Common Law Employee?

Under common-law rules, anyone who performs services for you is your employee if you can control what will be done and how it will be done. This is so even when you give the employee freedom of action. What matters is that you have the right to control the details of how the services are performed.

To determine whether an individual is an employee or independent contractor under the common law, the relationship of the worker and the business must be examined. All evidence of control and independence must be considered. In an employee/independent contractor determination, all information that provides evidence of the degree of control and degree of independence must be considered.

Facts that provide evidence of the degree of control and independence fall into three categories: behavioral control, financial control and the type of relationship between the parties. Refer to Publication 15-A, Employer's Supplemental Tax Guide for additional information.

Defining Who Is an Employee

A general rule is that anyone who performs services for you is your employee if you can control what will be done and how it will be done.

Example

Donna Lee is a salesperson employed on a full-time basis by Bob Blue, an auto dealer. She works 6 days a week and is on duty in Bob's showroom on certain assigned days and times. She appraises trade-ins, but her appraisals are subject to the sales manager's approval. Lists of prospective customers belong to the dealer. She has to develop leads and report results to the sales manager. Because of her experience, she requires only minimal assistance in closing and financing sales and in other phases of her work. She is paid a commission and is eligible for prizes and bonuses offered by Bob. Bob also pays the cost of health insurance and group-term life insurance for Donna. Donna is an employee of Bob Blue.

What Is a Statutory Employee?

If workers are independent contractors under the common-law rules, such workers may nevertheless be treated as employees by statute for certain employment tax purposes if they fall within any one of the following four categories and meet the three conditions described under Social Security and Medicare taxes.

1. a driver who distributes beverages other than milk or meat, vegetable, fruit or bakery products, or who picks up and delivers laundry or dry cleaning, if the driver is your agent or is paid on commission

2. a full-time life insurance sales agent whose principal business activity is selling life insurance or annuity contracts, or both, primarily for one life insurance company

3. an individual who works at home on materials or goods that you supply and that must be returned to you or to a person you name, if you also furnish specifications for the work to be done

4. a full-time traveling or city salesperson who works on your behalf and turns in orders to you from wholesalers, retailers, contractors, or operators of hotels, restaurants or other similar establishments (The goods sold must be merchandise for resale or supplies for use in the buyer's business operation. The work performed for you must be the salesperson's principal business activity. Refer to the Salesperson section of Publication 15-A, Employer's Supplemental Tax Guide, for additional information.)

Statutory Nonemployees

There are two categories of statutory nonemployees: direct sellers and licensed real estate agents. They are treated as self-employed for all federal tax purposes, including income and employment taxes, if:

- substantially all payments for their services as direct sellers or real estate agents are directly related to sales or other output, rather than to the number of hours worked; and

- their services are performed under a written contract providing that they will not be treated as employees for federal tax purposes.

Refer to information on direct sellers located in Publication 15-A, Employer's Supplemental Tax Guide, for additional information.

Misclassification of Employees

Consequences of Treating an Employee as an Independent Contractor

If you classify an employee as an independent contractor and you have no reasonable basis for doing so, you may be held liable for employment taxes for that worker. See Internal Revenue Code Section 3509 for additional information.

Most businesses start out small. As a new business owner, you need to know your federal tax responsibilities. The following sections provide links to basic federal tax information for people who are starting a business. It also provides information to assist in making basic business decisions. The list should not be construed as all-inclusive. Other steps may be appropriate for your specific type of business.

Business Taxes

The form of business that you operate determines what taxes you must pay and how you must pay them. The following are the four general types of business taxes:

- income tax
- self-employment tax
- employment taxes
- excise tax

All businesses, except partnerships, must file an annual income tax return. Partnerships file an information return. The form you use depends on how your business is organized.

The federal income tax is a pay-as-you-go tax. You must pay the tax as you earn or receive income during the year. An employee usually has income tax withheld from his or her pay. If you do not pay your tax through withholding or do not pay enough tax that way, you might have to pay estimated tax. If you are not required to make estimated tax payments, you may pay any tax due when you file your return. For additional information refer to Publication 583, Starting a Business and Keeping Records.

Self-Employment Tax

Self-employment (SE) tax is a Social Security and Medicare tax primarily for individuals who work for themselves. Your payments of SE tax contribute to your coverage under the Social Security system. Social Security coverage provides you with retirement benefits, disability benefits, survivor benefits and hospital insurance (Medicare) benefits.

You must pay SE tax and file Schedule SE (Form 1040) if either of the following applies:

- your net earnings from self-employment were $400 or more; or
- you had church employee income of $108.28 or more.

For additional information, visit www.irs.gov and refer to the Self-Employment Tax page.

Employment Taxes

When you have employees, you have certain employment tax responsibilities that you must pay and forms you must file as the employer. Employment taxes include the following:

- Social Security and Medicare taxes
- federal income tax withholding
- FUTA tax

For additional information, visit www.irs.gov and refer to the Employment Taxes for Small Businesses page.

Excise Tax

Excise taxes are taxes paid when purchases are made on a specific good, such as gasoline. Excise taxes are often included in the price of the product. There are also excise taxes on activities, such as on wagering or on highway usage by trucks. Excise tax has several general programs. One of the major components of the excise program is motor fuel. For additional information, visit www.irs.gov and refer to the Excise Taxes page.

The Importance of Good Record Keeping

Everyone in business must keep records. Keeping good records is very important to your business. Good records will help you do the following:

- monitor the progress of your business
- prepare your financial statements
- identify source of receipts
- keep track of deductible expenses
- prepare your tax returns
- support items reported on tax returns

You need good records to monitor the progress of your business. Records can show whether your business is improving, which items are selling or what changes you need to make. Good records can increase the likelihood of business success.

Prepare Your Financial Statements

You need good records to prepare accurate financial statements. These include income, or profit and loss, statements and balance sheets. These statements can help you in dealing with your bank or creditors and help you manage your business.

- An income statement shows the income and expenses of the business for a given period of time.
- A balance sheet shows the assets, liabilities and your equity in the business on a given date.

Identify Source of Receipts

You will receive money or property from many sources. Your records can identify the source of your receipts. You need this information to separate business from nonbusiness receipts and taxable from nontaxable income.

Keep Track of Deductible Expenses

You may forget expenses when you prepare your tax return, unless you record them when they occur.

Prepare Your Tax Return

You need good records to prepare your tax returns. These records must support the income, expenses and credits you report. Generally, these are the same records you use to monitor your business and prepare your financial statement.

Support Items Reported on Tax Returns

You must keep your business records available at all times for inspection by the IRS. If the IRS examines any of your tax returns, you may be asked to explain the items reported. A complete set of records will speed up the examination.

You may choose any record-keeping system suited to your business that clearly shows your income. Except in a few cases, the law does not require any special kinds of records. However, the business you are in affects the types of records that you need to keep for federal tax purposes. Your record-keeping system should also include a summary of your business transactions. This summary is ordinarily made in your business books—for example, accounting journals and ledgers. Your books must show your gross income as well as your deductions and credits. For most small businesses, the business checkbook is the main source for entries in the business books.

Supporting Business Documents

Purchases, sales, payroll and other transactions you have in your business will generate supporting documents, such as invoices and receipts. Supporting documents include sales slips, paid bills, invoices, receipts, deposit slips and canceled checks. These documents contain the information you need to record in your books. It is important to keep these documents because they support the entries in your books and on your tax return. You should keep them in an orderly fashion and in a safe place. For instance, organize them by year and type of income or expense. For more detailed information, refer to Publication 583, Starting a Business and Keeping Records.

The following are some of the types of records you should keep:

Gross Receipts

Gross receipts are the income you receive from your business. You should keep supporting documents that show the amounts and sources of your gross receipts. Documents for gross receipts include the following:

- cash register tapes
- receipt books
- credit card charge slips
- bank deposit slips
- invoices
- Forms 1099-MISC

Purchases

Purchases are the items you buy and resell to customers. If you are a manufacturer or producer, this includes the cost of all raw materials or parts purchased for manufacture into finished products. Your supporting documents should show the amount paid and that the amount was for purchases. Documents for purchases include the following:

- canceled checks
- credit card sales slips
- cash register tape receipts
- invoices

Expenses

Expenses are the costs you incur–other than purchases–to carry on your business. Your supporting documents should show the amount paid and that the amount was for a business expense. Documents for expenses include the following:

- canceled checks
- account statements
- invoices
- cash register tapes
- credit card sales slips
- petty cash slips for small cash payments

Travel, Transportation, Entertainment and Gift Expenses

If you deduct travel, entertainment, gift or transportation expenses, you must be able to prove, or substantiate, certain elements of expenses. For additional information on how to prove certain business expenses, refer to Publication 463, Travel, Entertainment, Gift and Car Expenses.

Hint

Assets are the property–such as machinery and furniture–that you own and use in your business. You must keep records to verify certain information about your business assets. You need records to compute the annual depreciation and the gain or loss when you sell the assets.

Recording Business Transactions

A good record-keeping system includes a summary of your business transactions. Business transactions are ordinarily summarized in books called journals and ledgers. You can buy them at your local stationery or office supply store. A journal is a book where you record each business transaction shown in your supporting documents. You may have to keep separate journals for transactions that occur frequently.

There are specific employment tax records that you must keep. Keep all records of employment for at least 4 years. A ledger is a book that contains the totals from all of your journals. It is organized into different accounts.

Whether you keep journals and ledgers and how you keep them depends on the type of business you are in. For example, a record-keeping system for a small business might include the following items:

- business checkbook
- monthly summary of cash receipts
- depreciation worksheet
- daily summary of cash receipts
- check disbursements journal
- employee compensation records

Note

The system you use to record business transactions will be more effective if you follow good record-keeping practices. For example, record expenses when they occur and identify the source of recorded receipts. Generally, it is best to record transactions on a daily basis.

Keep all records of employment taxes for at least 4 years. These should be available for IRS review. Records should include:

- your EIN
- amounts and dates of all wage, annuity and pension payments
- amounts of tips reported
- the fair market value of in-kind wages paid
- names, addresses, Social Security numbers and occupations of employees and recipients
- any employee copies of Form W-2 that were returned to you as undeliverable
- dates of employment
- periods for which employees and recipients were paid while absent due to sickness or injury and the amount and weekly rate of payments that you or third-party payers made to them
- copies of employees' and recipients' income tax withholding allowance certificates (Forms W-4, W-4P, W-4S, and W-4V)
- dates and amounts of tax deposits you made
- copies of returns filed
- records of allocated tips
- records of fringe benefits provided, including substantiation
- Occupational Safety and Health Administration records

Every employer covered by OSHA who has more than 10 employees—except for employers in certain low-hazard industries such as retail, finance, insurance, real estate and some service industries—must maintain OSHA-specified records of job-related injuries and illnesses.

Burden of Proof

The responsibility to prove entries, deductions and statements made on your tax returns is known as the burden of proof. You must be able to prove, or substantiate, certain elements of expenses in order to deduct them. Generally, taxpayers meet their burden of proof by having the information and receipts for the expenses where needed. You should keep adequate records to prove your expenses or have sufficient evidence that will support your own statement. You generally must have documentary evidence, such as receipts, canceled checks or bills to support your expenses.

The length of time you should keep a document depends on the action, expense or event the document records. Generally, you must keep records that support an item of income or deductions on a tax return until the period of limitations for that return runs out.

The time you are required to keep records includes the period of time during which you can amend your tax return to claim a credit or refund or the period of time that the IRS can assess more tax. You should also keep copies of your filed tax returns in the following 10 situations:

1. You owe additional tax and situations 2, 3 and 4, (below) do not apply to you; keep records for 3 years.
2. You do not report income that you should report, and it is more than 25 percent of the gross income shown on your return; keep records for 6 years.
3. You file a fraudulent income tax return; keep records indefinitely.
4. You do not file a return; keep records indefinitely.
5. You file a claim for credit or refund after you file your return; keep records for 2 to 3 years after tax was paid.
6. Your claim is due to a bad debt deduction; keep records for 7 years.
7. Your claim is due to a loss from worthless securities; keep records for 7 years.
8. Keep information on an asset for the life of the asset, even when you dispose of the asset; keep records indefinitely.
9. Keep all employment tax records for at least 4 years after the date that the tax becomes due or is paid, whichever is later.
10. The following criteria should be applied to each record as you decide whether to keep a document or throw it away: a. Keep records relating to property until the period of limitations expires for the year in which you dispose of the property in a taxable disposition. You must keep these records to figure any depreciation, amortization or depletion deduction and to figure the gain or loss when you sell or otherwise dispose of the property. b. When your records are no longer needed for tax purposes, do not discard them until you check to see if you have to keep them longer for other purposes. For example, your insurance company or creditors may require you to keep them longer than the IRS does.

Resources

Free Publications Available From the IRS

Publication 535, Business Expenses

Publication 536, Net Operating Losses

Publication 547, Casualties, Disasters and Thefts (business and nonbusiness)

Publication 594, IRS Collection Process

Publication 583, Starting a Business and Keeping Records

Publication 334, Tax Guide for Small Business

Tax Topic 762 Basic Information

To determine whether a worker is an independent contractor or an employee, you must examine the relationship between the worker and the business. All evidence of control and independence in this relationship should be considered. The facts that provide this evidence fall into three categories: behavioral control, financial control and the type of relationship itself.

Publication 1976, Section 530, Employment Tax Relief Requirements, provides businesses with relief from federal employment tax obligations if certain requirements are met.

IRS Internal Training: Employee/Independent Contractor

This manual provides you with the tools to make correct determinations of worker classifications. It discusses facts that may indicate the existence of an independent contractor or an employer-employee relationship. This training manual is a guide and is not legally binding.

Form SS-8

If you would like the IRS to make the determination of worker status, file IRS Form SS-8, Determination of Worker Status for Purposes of Federal Employment Taxes and Income Tax Withholding.

Publication 15-A

Publication 15-A, The Employer's Supplemental Tax Guide, has detailed guidance, including information for specific industries.

Publication 15-B

Publication 15-B, The Employer's Tax Guide to Fringe Benefits, supplements Publication 15, (Circular E), Employer's Tax Guide and Publication 15-A, Employer's Supplemental Tax Guide. It contains specialized and detailed information on the employment tax treatment of fringe benefits.

Pulling It All Together

Determine If It Is a Business or a Hobby

Use this checklist to determine if your business is a business or a hobby.

_____ Your business is expected to show a profit.

_____ You can expect to make a future profit from the appreciation of the assets used in the activity.

_____ You carry on the activity in a businesslike manner.

_____ The time and effort you put into the activity indicate that you intend to make it profitable.

_____ You depend on income from the activity for your livelihood.

_____ Your losses are due to circumstances beyond your control or are normal in the startup phase of your type of business.

_____ You change your methods of operation in an attempt to improve profitability.

_____ You or your advisors have the knowledge needed to carry on the activity as a successful business.

_____ You were successful in making a profit in similar activities in the past.

_____ The activity makes a profit in some years and varies in the amount of profit it makes.

_____ You have obtained an EIN.

Keep Track of Your Taxes:

- Declare your fiscal year end date.
- Set up a tax filing calendar.
- Hire an accountant to prepare your tax statements.
- Keep all business transaction and employee records for a minimum of 5 years.

Finally, when your records are no longer needed for tax purposes, do not discard them until you check to see if you have to keep them longer for other purposes. For example, your insurance company or creditors may require you to keep them longer than the IRS does.

21 Great Resources for Small Businesses

Library Resources

Indexes to periodicals and magazine articles

Inc.
  http://inc.com

Fast Company
  www.fastcompany.com

CFO
  www.cfo.com/cfo_home

Time
  www.time.com

BusinessWeek
  www.businessweek.com

Fortune
  www.fortune.com/fortune

Forbes
  www.forbes.com

Newsweek
  www.msnbc.com/news/NW.front_Front.asp

Entrepreneur
  http://entrepreneur.com

Bizjournals
  www.bizjournals.com

Startup Journal
  www.startupjournal.com

Business Resource Links

Business Owner's Toolkit
http://toolkit.cch.com

Entreworld
www.entreworld.org

CEOExpress
www.ceoexpress.com/default.asp

Yahoo! Small Business
http://smallbusiness.yahoo.com

U.S. Chamber of Commerce
www.uschamber.com/default

American Express Small Business
http://home3.americanexpress.com/smallbusiness/tool/biz_plan/index.asp

Quicken Small Business
www.quicken.com/small_business

Small Business Research Portal
www.smallbusinessportal.co.uk/nmegasites.htm

eWeb
http://eweb.slu.edu/Default.htm

Canada Business
http://canadabusiness.gc.ca/gol/cbec/site.nsf

Microsoft Small Business Center
www.microsoft.com/smallbusiness/resources/articles.mspx

itsSimple.biz State Resource Centers
www.itssimple.biz/resource_center

eBiz Training Catalog
www.sbasupport.org/ebtdc/asp/sp_training.asp

U.S. Government Departments

www.business.gov

The official business link to the U.S. government—includes information about:

• business statistics	• employment data
• trade statistics	• market research
• country data	• publications by agency
• business publications	• environment

www.firstgov.gov

The U.S. government's official Web portal

www.irs.gov/businesses/small

Small business and self.employed one.stop resource

www.sba.gov

U.S. Small Business Administration

www.sba.gov/library/pubs.html#fm.8

U.S. Small Business Administration publications library

Associations

www.score.org

The Service Corps of Retired Executives

SCORE is a nonprofit group of mostly retired businesspeople who volunteer to provide counseling to small businesses at no charge. A program of the SBA, SCORE has been around since 1964 and has helped more than three million entrepreneurs and aspiring entrepreneurs. SCORE is a source for all kinds of business advice, from how to write a business plan to investigating marketing potential and managing cash flow. SCORE counselors work out of nearly 400 local chapters throughout the United States. You can obtain a referral to a counselor in your local chapter by contacting the national office.

www.nbia.com

National Business Incubation Association

The NBIA is the national organization for business incubators, which are organizations specially set up to nurture young firms and help them survive and grow. Incubators provide leased office facilities on flexible terms, shared business services, management assistance and help in obtaining financing and technical support. NBIA says there are nearly 600 incubators in North America. Its services include providing a directory of local incubators and their services.

www.uschamber.com/default

U.S. Chamber of Commerce

The many chambers of commerce throughout the United States are organizations devoted to providing networking, lobbying, training and more. If you think chambers are all about having lunch with a bunch of community boosters, think again. Among the services the U.S. Chamber of Commerce offers is a Web based business solutions program that provides online help with specific small business needs, including planning; marketing; creating a press release, collecting a bad debt, recruiting employees or creating a retirement plan.

The U.S. Chamber of Commerce is the umbrella organization for the more than 1,000 local chambers in the United States. If you plan on doing business overseas, do not forget to check for an American Chamber of Commerce in the countries where you hope to have a presence. They are set up to provide information and assistance to U.S. firms seeking to do business there. Many, but not all, countries have American chambers.

SBA Development Centers

Anchorage, AK District Office
510 L St., Suite 310
Anchorage, AK 99501
Telephone: 1.907.271.4022

Alabama District Office
801 Tom Martin Dr., Suite #201
Birmingham, AL 35211
Telephone: 1.205.290.7101
Fax: 1.205.290.7404

Arkansas District Office
2120 Riverfront Dr., Suite 250
Little Rock, AR 72202
Telephone: 1.501.324.5871
Fax: 1.501.324.5199

Arizona District Office
2828 N. Central Ave., Suite 800
Phoenix, AZ 85004
Telephone: 1.602.745.7200
Fax: 1.602.745.7210

Fresno District Office
2719 N. Air Fresno Dr., Suite 200
Fresno, CA 93727
Telephone: 1.559.487.5791
Fax: 1.559.487.5636

Los Angeles District Office
330 N. Brand, Suite 1200
Glendale, CA 91203
Telephone: 1.818.552.3215

Sacramento District Office
650 Capitol Mall, Suite 7.500
Sacramento, CA 95814
Telephone: 1.916.930.3700
Fax: 1.916.930.3737

San Diego District Office
550 W. C St., Suite 550
San Diego, CA 92101
Telephone: 1.619.557.7250
Fax: 1.619.557.5894
TTY: 1.619.557.6998

San Francisco District Office
455 Market St., Sixth Floor
San Francisco, CA 94105
Telephone: 1.415.744.6820

Santa Ana District Office
200 W Santa Ana Blvd., Suite 700
Santa Ana, CA 92701
Telephone: 1.714.550.7420
TTY/TDD: 1.714.550.0655

Colorado District Office
721 19th St., Suite 426
Denver, CO 80202
Telephone: 1.303.844.2607

Connecticut District Office
330 Main St., Second Floor
Hartford, CT 06106
Telephone: 1.860.240.4700

Washington, D.C. District Office
1110 Vermont Ave. N.W., Ninth Floor
Washington, D.C. 20005
Telephone: 1.202.606.4000

Wilmington, DE District Office
824 N. Market St., Suite 610
Wilmington, DE 19801
Telephone: 1.302.573.6294

North Florida District Office
7825 Baymeadows Way, Suite 100B
Jacksonville, FL 32256
Telephone: 1.904.443.1900

South Florida District Office
100 S. Biscayne Blvd., Seventh Floor
Miami, FL 33131
Telephone: 1.305.536.5521
Fax: 1.305.536.5058

Georgia District Office
233 Peachtree St. N.E., Suite 1900
Atlanta, GA 30303
Telephone: 1.404.331.0100

Guam Branch Office
400 Route 8, Suite 302
First Hawaiian Bank Building
Mongmong, GU 96927
Telephone: 1.671.472.7419
Fax: 1.671.472.7365

Hawaii District Office
300 Ala Moana Blvd., Room 2.235
P.O. Box 50207
Honolulu, HI 96850
Telephone: 1.808.541.2990
Fax: 1.808.541.2976

Des Moines Office
210 Walnut St., Room 749
Des Moines, IA 50309
Telephone: 1.515.284.4422

Cedar Rapids Office
215 Fourth Ave. S.E., Suite 200
Cedar Rapids, IA 52401
Telephone: 1.319.362.6405

Boise District Office
380 East Parkcenter Blvd., Suite 330
Boise, ID 83706
Telephone: 1.208.334.6963
Fax: 1.208.334.9353

Illinois District Office
500 W. Madison St., Suite 1250
Chicago, IL 60661
Telephone: 1.312.353.4528

Indiana District Office
429 N. Pennsylvania St., Suite 100
Indianapolis, IN 46204
Telephone: 1.317.226.7272

Kansas District Office
271 W. Third St., N. Suite 2500
Wichita, KS 67202
Telephone: 1.316.269.6616

Kentucky District Office
600 Dr. MLK Jr. Pl.
Louisville, KY 40202
Telephone: 1.502.582.5971

New Orleans District Office
365 Canal St., Suite 2820
New Orleans, LA 70130
Telephone: 1.504.589.6685

Massachusetts District Office
10 Causeway St., Room 265
Boston, MA 02222
Telephone: 1.617.565.5590

Maryland District Office
City Crescent Building, Sixth Floor
10 S. Howard St.
Baltimore, MD 21201
Telephone: 1.410.962.4392

Maine District Office
Edmund S. Muskie Federal Building,
Room 512
68 Sewall St.
Augusta, ME 04330
Telephone: 1.207.622.8274

Michigan District Office
477 Michigan Ave., Suite 515
McNamara Building
Detroit, MI 48226
Telephone: 1.313.226.6075

Minneapolis, MN District Office
100 N. Sixth St.
Suite 210.C Butler Square
Minneapolis, MN 55403
Telephone: 1.612.370.2324
Fax: 1.612.370.2303

Kansas City District Office
323 W. Eighth St., Suite 501
Kansas City, MO 64105
Telephone: 1.816.374.6701

Mississippi District Office
AmSouth Bank Plaza
210 E. Capitol St., Suite 900
Jackson, MS 39201
Telephone: 1.601.965.4378
Fax: 1.601.965.5629 or
1.601.965.4294

Gulfport Branch Office
Hancock Bank Plaza
2510 14th St., Suite 101
Gulfport, MS 39501
Telephone: 1.228.863.4449
Fax: 1.228.864.0179

Montana District Office
10 W. 15th St., Suite 1100
Helena, MT 59626
Telephone: 1.406.441.1081
Fax: 1.406.441.1090

North Carolina District Office
6302 Fairview Rd., Suite 300
Charlotte, NC 28210
Telephone: 1.704.344.6563
Fax: 1.704.344.6769

North Dakota District Office
657 Second Ave. N., Room 219
Fargo, ND 58102
Telephone: 1.701.239.5131

Nebraska District Office
11145 Mill Valley Rd.
Omaha, NE 68154
Telephone: 1.402.221.4691

New Hampshire District Office
JC Cleveland Federal Building
55 Pleasant St., Suite 3101
Concord, NH 03301
Telephone: 1.603.225.1400
Fax: 1.603.225.1409

New Jersey District Office
Two Gateway Center, 15th Floor
Newark, NJ 07102
Telephone: 1.973.645.2434

Albuquerque District Office
625 Silver S.W., Suite 320
Albuquerque, NM 87102
Telephone: 1.505.346.7909
Fax: 1.505.346.6711

Nevada District Office
400 S. Fourth St., Suite 250
Las Vegas, NV 89101
Telephone: 1.702.388.6611
Fax: 1.702.388.6469

Buffalo District Office
111 W. Huron St., Suite 1311
Buffalo, NY 14202
Telephone: 1.716.551.4301
Fax: 1.716.551.4418

New York District Office
26 Federal Plaza, Suite 3100
New York, NY 10278
Telephone: 1.212.264.4354
Fax: 1.212.264.4963

Syracuse District Office
401 S. Salina St., Fifth Floor
Syracuse, NY 13202
Telephone: 1.315.471.9393
Fax: 1.315.471.9288

Cleveland, OH District Office
1350 Euclid Ave., Suite 211
Cleveland, OH 44115
Telephone: 1.216.522.4180
Fax: 1.216.522.2038
TDD: 1.216.522.8350

Columbus, OH District Office
2 Nationwide Plaza, Suite 1400
Columbus, OH 43215
Telephone: 1.614.469.6860

Oklahoma City District Office
Federal Building
301 N.W. Sixth St.
Oklahoma City, OK 73102
Telephone: 1.405.609.8000

Portland, OR District Office
601 S.W. Second Ave., Suite 950
Portland, OR 97204
Telephone: 1.503.326.2682
Fax: 1.503.326.2808

Philadelphia District Office
Robert N.C. Nix Federal Building
900 Market St., Fifth Floor
Philadelphia, PA 19107
Telephone: 1.215.580.2SBA

Pittsburgh District Office
411 Seventh Ave., Suite 1450
Pittsburgh, PA 15219
Telephone: 1.412.395.6560

Puerto Rico and U.S. Virgin Islands
District Office
252 Ponce de Leon Ave.
Citibank Tower, Suite 201
Hato Rey, PR 00918
Telephone: 1.787.766.5572 or
1.800.669.8049
Fax: 1.787.766.5309

Rhode Island District Office
380 Westminster St., Room 511
Providence, RI 02903
Telephone: 1.401.528.4561

South Carolina District Office
1835 Assembly St., Room 1425
Columbia, SC 29201
Telephone: 1.803.765.5377
Fax: 1.803.765.5962

South Dakota District Office
2329 N. Career Ave., Suite 105
Sioux Falls, SD 57107
Telephone: 1.605.330.4243
Fax: 1.605.330.4215
TTY/TDD: 1.605.331.3527

Tennessee District Office
50 Vantage Way, Suite 201
Nashville, TN 37228
Telephone: 1.615.736.5881
Fax: 1.615.736.7232
TTY/TDD: 1.615.736.2499

Dallas District Office
4300 Amon Carter Blvd., Suite 114
Fort Worth, TX 76155
Telephone: 1.817.684.5500
Fax: 1.817.684.5516

El Paso District Office
10737 Gateway West
El Paso, TX 79935
Telephone: 1.915.633.7001
Fax: 1.915.633.7005

Harlingen District Office
222 E. Van Buren St., Suite 500
Harlingen, TX 78550
Telephone: 1.956.427.8533

Corpus Christi Branch Office
3649 Leopard St., Suite 411
Corpus Christi, TX 78408
Telephone: 1.361.879.0017

Houston District Office
8701 S. Gessner Dr., Suite 1200
Houston, TX 77074
Telephone: 1.713.773.6500
Fax: 1.713.773.6550

Lubbock District Office
1205 Texas Ave., Room 408
Lubbock, TX 79401
Telephone: 1.806.472.7462
Fax: 1.806.472.7487

San Antonio District Office
17319 San Pedro, Suite 200
San Antonio, TX 78232
Telephone: 1.210.403.5900
Fax: 1.210.403.5936
TDD: 1.210.403.5933

Utah District Office
125 S. State St., Room 2231
Salt Lake City, UT 84138
Telephone: 1.801.524.3209

Richmond, VA District Office
400 N. Eighth St.
Federal Building, Suite 1150
Richmond, VA 23240
Telephone: 1.804.771.2400
Fax: 1.804.771.2764

Vermont District Office
87 State St., Room 205
Montpelier, VT 05601
Telephone: 1.802.828.4422

Seattle, WA District Office
1200 Sixth Ave., Suite 1700
Corner of Sixth and University
Seattle, WA 98101
Telephone: 1.206.553.7310

Spokane, WA Branch Office
801 W. Riverside Ave., Suite 200
Spokane, WA 99201
Telephone: 1.509.353.2811

Wisconsin District Office
740 Regent St., Suite 100
Madison, WI 53715
Telephone: 1.608.441.5263
Fax: 1.608.441.5541

310 W. Wisconsin Ave., Room 400
Milwaukee, WI 53203
Telephone: 1.414.297.3941
Fax: 1.414.297.1377

West Virginia District Office
320 W. Pike St., Suite 330
Clarksburg, WV 26301
Telephone: 1.304.623.5631

Wyoming District Office
100 E. B St.
Federal Building
P.O. Box 44001
Casper, WY 82602
Telephone: 1.307.261.6500

Online Data Providers

Data Providers

Use for obtaining statistics and tables and for identifying potential sources for data.

Experian: Credit reporting bureau
  www.experian.com

Hoovers: Data for virtually every company
  www.hoovers.com

U.S. Census Bureau
  www.census.gov

U. S. Department of Commerce: Bureau of Economic Analysis
  www.bea.gov

U.S. Department of Labor: Bureau of Labor Statistics
  www.bls.gov

Federal Reserve Economic Data (FRED)
  http://research.stlouisfed.org/fred2

Federal Statistical Agencies
  www.fedstats.gov/agencies/agencies.html

FedStats
  www.fedstats.gov

National Bureau of Economic Research
  www.nber.org/data

National Center for Health Statistics
  www.cdc.gov/nchs

New York City Department of City Planning
  http://home.nyc.gov/html/dcp/html/subcats/resources.html

New York State Data Centers
  www.nylovesbiz.com/nysdc/default.asp

U.S. Census Bureau State Data Centers
  www.census.gov/sdc/www

Population Data

Data Extractors

Use for building data tables suitable for downloading.

American FactFinder
http://factfinder.census.gov/home/saff/main.html?_lang=en

Data Access Tools for U.S. Census Data
www.census.gov/main/www/access.html

Integrated Public Use Microdata Series 1.IPUMS.
www.ipums.umn.edu

U.S. Historical Census Data Browser
http://fisher.lib.virginia.edu/collections/stats/histcensus

1990 Census Lookup at University of California, Berkeley
http://goldrush.berkeley.edu/GovData/info

Data Resources at Center for International Earth Science Information Network
1.CIESIN.
www.ciesin.org/data.html

Global Environmental Outlook
http://gridca.grid.unep.ch/geoportal/index2.php

Networked Social Science Tools and Resources 1.NESSTAR.
www.nesstar.com

Survey Documentation and Analysis 1.SDA.Online Data Analysis System from the
Inter.University Consortium for Political and Social Research 1.ICPSR)
www.icpsr.umich.edu/access/sda.html

State Politics and Policy Quarterly Data Resources
www.unl.edu/SPPQ

TransStat: The Intermodal Transportation Database
www.transtats.bts.gov

Index

Limited Liability Companies Software (SS4309)

INCLUDES E-BOOK AND 10 FORMS.

All the instructions and forms you need to set up and manage your own Limited Liability Company, allowing you the tax advantages of a partnership and the liability protection of a corporation.

Partnerships Software (SS4310)

INCLUDES E-BOOK AND 11 FORMS.

Save time and money by learning how to set up and maintain an effective business partnership—from choosing the type that's right for you to obtaining financing and creating an agreement that satisfies all concerned.

Incorporation Kit (K325)

INCLUDES CD, INSTRUCTION MANUAL AND 20 FORMS.

Protect your personal assets from your business' liabilities by incorporating. Decide which type of corporation is best for you and handle the incorporation yourself using this comprehensive kit.

Small Business Home Business Kit (K321)

INCLUDES INSTRUCTION MANUAL AND 21 FORMS.

Be your own boss. With this convenient, comprehensive kit, you'll be able to set up your own business and achieve your personal goal of financial independence.